MICROFARMING
for PROFIT

from GARDEN *to* GLORY

First Torrey House Press Edition, January 2015
Copyright © 2015 by Dave DeWitt

Published by Torrey House Press, LLC
Salt Lake City, Utah
www.torreyhouse.com

International Standard Book Number: 978-1-937226-38-1
Library of Congress Control Number: 2014939594

Author photo by Sergio Salvador
Cover and interior design by Lois Manno

MICROFARMING
for PROFIT

from GARDEN *to* GLORY

Dave DeWitt

TORREY HOUSE PRESS, LLC

SALT LAKE CITY • TORREY

Selected Books by Dave DeWitt

The Pepper Garden
Peppers of the World
The Complete Chile Pepper Book
The Southwest Table
Dishing Up New Mexico
Too Many Chiles

CONTENTS

Acknowledgments

Thanks to everyone who assisted with this project: Marlin Bensinger, Mary Jane Wilan, Gillie Augeri, Leo Lascaux, Matt Yohalem, Ethan Diness, Kathi Caldwell, Lorenzo Candelaria, Hans Wressnig, all the microfarmers profiled or mentioned, and my long-time agent, Scott Mendel.

INTRODUCTION

The Great Terrarium

In 2013, I built my fourth microfarm, and that's one of the microfarms profiled in Part 4 of this book. My first was in Richmond, Virginia, when my wife at the time decided she wanted to open a retail, boutique plant shop in the trendy section of town called the Fan District. Terrariums were all the rage around 1970, and my wife wanted to take advantage of the craze. Like the gift baskets of today, she wanted to build the terrariums and sell them to people as gift items or decorations for homes. But first we had a whole lot to learn.

I was already a knowledgeable gardener — my parents had taken good care of that education. But neither my wife nor I knew much about houseplants, aside from the commonest ones. If we were going to sell houseplants in any form, we had to learn as much as possible about them. We soon came to realize that buying plants wholesale and selling them retail was only part of the solution. Raising our own plants in greenhouses from seeds or cuttings was a much better idea, so that's what we did. I didn't call it a microfarm, but it was because I was growing plants for money, not as a hobby. After six months of planning, studying, building a makeshift greenhouse, and growing most of the plants we could sell, my wife had the grand opening of The Great Terrarium. Of course, I produced the radio commercials for it, and business was brisk.

The shop was successful and profitable, but after a year, one big problem emerged: my wife didn't like being a retailer. She had to work weekends and late nights during sales. It was difficult to find good help, and even though she made money, she was not happy. So after one year, when the lease was up, she closed the business, paid all the bills, and went back to the profession she studied in college: interior design.

Forty-three years later, I'm still growing plants for money, but I don't depend on it for survival. It's just a hobby gone nuts, and it's mostly about chile peppers, which are my specialty, and interacting with the New Mexico food community, of which I am very much a part. Over the years, I've developed techniques to produce the highest possible yields. For the most part, I use organic methods but I'm not one hundred percent organic. I subscribe to the same philosophy as the late Dick Thompson, who was one of the founders of Practical Farmers of Iowa and practiced what he called "a more balanced farming system." He was one of the "beacons of sustainable agriculture," according to food expert Mark Bittman. He was not an organic farmer, but a practical one. He occasionally used herbicides when they were necessary, and I do too, but not directly in my microfarm. I use them only when weeds first sprout away from the microfarmed area so my yard will not be overwhelmed by fast-growing Russian thistles, commonly called tumbleweeds.

Thompson also assisted his compost by using chemical fertilizers. I do too, but only for the plants in pots with restricted roots. Otherwise they would have very low yields. I happen to believe that if the plant needs nitrogen, it doesn't matter how that element is applied. Plants in pots need a much higher amount than plants fertilized with manure that have much larger root systems, and a water-soluble source does an excellent job of fertilizer application. I do not use insecticides but rather inspect the plants closely using mechanical means, like directed streams of water and insect traps, to remove the pests. I handpick the tomato hornworms off my plants and feed them to the robins.

Dick Thompson and his wife had such a productive farm compared to his neighbors' monocultural farms with tons of chemicals, that from the mid '80s to his death in 2013, he and his wife showed more than forty thousand visitors how a relatively small farm could support a small family by respecting and caring for the land. His soil had twice the amount of organic material as his neighbors' and his farm yielded between $150 and $200 more per acre than the others. He didn't have a microfarm, but three hundred acres, which these days is called a small farm. Microfarmers would call it huge.

Mark Bittman, writing in the Opinionator column of *The New York Times*, wrote that Dick Thompson "tried to figure out a system that would work for the farmer, the land, the animals, and the customer." He succeeded, and I've succeeded in my own little way that is almost identical to his way, in micro form.

During the waning moments of World War II, my parents, like so many other families, had a Victory Garden, and at that non-supermarket time, Victory Gardens produced forty percent of all produce consumed in this country. That's because most of the food was being preserved and sent to our forces in Europe and the Pacific. Home bottling and canning probably reached their all-time peak.

And, of course, my parents were unconsciously brainwashing us to believe that home gardens were patriotic and therefore our duty. Later, when my brother Rick and I were the year-after-year garden grunts of our parents' backyard growing projects in the 1950s, we jokingly referred to each one of the gardens as another Victory Garden. Not victory for our country, but for our family. And we didn't need to do it for the money, but if times had been tough, the whole family would have expanded our Victory Garden into a profitable microfarm. No doubt about it.

What Is a Microfarmer, Anyway?

The term "garden" indicates hobby-growing to me while "farm" and "ranch" refer to growing with the goal of making a profit. So, to my way of thinking, a large garden and a microfarm could be identical except for their purposes. A microfarmer does have a fair amount of land, usually between one-quarter of an acre and a maximum of five acres and is growing to make money, not just for a hobby or to feed the family. People who grow ginseng, cow milk for cheese, oysters, oyster mushrooms, superhot chile peppers, garlic, blue corn, killer bee honey, medical marijuana, or other surprising crops. These are the microfarmers.

PART 1

PLANNING *your* MICROFARM

If you're seriously considering starting a microfarm, I have a few preliminary questions for you.

What are you trying to accomplish? If you're thinking that a microfarm can support your entire family, you'd better change the plan to a macrofarm, because that's unlikely to happen. It is better to think of microfarming as an enhancement to what income you already have, and that's why I recommend it for retirees, people who work from home already (like writers), or entrepreneurs who will use the microfarm to supply the basic goods for food products they manufacture.

Do you have time to farm? No, this is not a trick question. Spread out over the entire growing season, I estimate that I spent two hours a day maintaining my microfarm in 2013. But since the summer days are long, many of those hours can happen before 9 a.m. or after 5 p.m., and you can always catch up on weekends if you have a real job.

What do you like to grow, or want to grow? My father taught me how to grow tomatoes more than sixty years ago, and I'm still doing it. It's a crop I love to grow and I'm good at it, so it made sense for me to experiment with tomatoes first. Or, there could be a crop out there that you've always wanted to grow, like mushrooms or medical marijuana. My point here is that you have to be motivated by growing something you like and have the desire to grow it, and grow it well.

What is your skill/knowledge level? This book is not a guide to growing microfarm crops, but rather a guide to help you decide whether or not to farm, and if you decide to do it, helping you formulate a plan of action. Experience is always helpful, but it is not necessary. For example, Leo Lascaux, whose story is in Part 2, had never grown any plant before in his life. Yet he made a profit his first year of growing medical marijuana, and it was a significant one.

What do you know about running a business? This is actually more important than having gardening skills, because a microfarm is a business, not a garden. If you've never been an entrepreneur before, there are many books and courses on the subject. This is a microfarm-specific guide, so I recommend that you find a basic book on entrepreneurship and study it. Check out the last part of this book, Suggested Reading.

Where would you grow your microfarm crops? Unless you're growing medical marijuana, your microfarm does not have to be on your own property. Fields and farms are often leased to other growers, and many arrangements of that nature can be made. There are some greenhouse operators who shut down greenhouses during the winter because they don't grow crops or bedding plants in them, and if you can convince the owner that you can handle the tasks and pay the lease fee, you'll have expanded your microfarm dramatically into the winter months. Also, many cities and towns have community garden plots available for rent, although you may have to drive to them on a daily basis to care for your crops.

Are you physically fit for gardening? Although gardening and microfarming don't necessarily involve backbreaking labor, you have to be fit enough to lug around sacks of manure and potting soil, move some large pots with a hand truck, chop weeds sometimes, dig holes, mix and rake the garden after rototilling, and that sort of labor. If you suffer from any ailments that would prevent this work, you should think of another project or find a worker bee to help you.

Do you mind doing manual labor or repetitive tasks? In the sun? Some people find gardening work boring and just can't keep their focus on it. I think of it as exercise outdoors that will result in either cash or delicious meals or both, and don't even worry about the repetitive labor. Besides, there's always a bunch of things that need work on a microfarm, so water for a while, then harvest some tomatoes, check for weeds, water some more. Vary your tasks and give yourself rewards along the way—take a break for a beer, for example. Get all of your tasks done early, like before 9 a.m., and the sun will not be a problem.

Writing a Simple Business Plan

The purpose of writing a business plan is to formalize your ideas for a business by getting organized. If you are seeking financing or business partners, a written plan is a great start. By showing your plan to business people—like bankers, lawyers, and other business owners—you will receive valuable feedback and sometimes good advice. Business plans are not set in stone and you will be amazed to look back at your plan after concluding the first year of your microfarm and see how much it's already changed. Over time you will amend and revise your business plan because you cannot predict the future with perfect success. Here are eight steps outlining how to write a plan. Be succinct and keep the plan short and to the point.

1. **The Plan.** Outline the overall plan for your business. Specify what you are creating and write down what you think your business will be like in one, three, and five years.

2. **The Mission.** State why you are starting this business and what its purpose is.

3. **The Goals.** List your most important business goals and state how you will measure your success in achieving those goals.

4. **The Strategies.** Specify how you are going to build this business. Define what you will be selling and what your unique selling proposition is. In other words, what makes your business different from the competition?

5. **The Funding.** Estimate and break down the startup capital you will need to launch your business and state the source(s) of your funding.

6. **The Expenses.** Estimate your microfarm's monthly ongoing expenses upon launch, in three months, six months, and a year.

7. **The Income.** Estimate your microfarm's ongoing monthly income upon launch, in three months, six months, and a year.

8. **The Action.** Outline the actions you need to take now to get started. Set a number of future milestones, like what you hope to achieve in three months, six months, and a year. Then specify what actions you need to take to accomplish those milestones.

Remember to review and revise your plan periodically during your first year in business.

Determining Your Business Structure

It is important to examine the possible structures of your microfarm in order to decide which is best suited to you and your family. Pick the simplest structure that provides the most protection from risk. You should discuss these options with your attorney or other business advisors, like your accountant.

Sole Proprietorship

Definition: This is the simplest and one of the most common structures. The business, even with a trade name, is an extension of you. You own it, you run it, you receive all the income and are

Conduct your research to formulate a structure for your microfarm and a business plan.

personally responsible for the debts, losses, and liabilities. Freelance writing is a good example of a sole proprietorship.

Formation: You don't have to take any action to form a sole proprietorship, but of course you are subject to all the laws, regulations, licenses, and permits that would apply to any other business structure.

Taxes: In a sole proprietorship, the business income is part of your personal income. Along with your regular personal income tax, you would file a Schedule C (Profit or Loss from Business— Sole Proprietorship) and transfer the bottom line of that form to your personal income tax form.

Advantages: This structure is inexpensive and easy to form, you have total control of the business, and taxes are simple to file.

Disadvantages: You will be held responsible for all obligations, debts, and other liabilities of the business, including those related to any employees you may have. Since you can't sell any interest in the business, including stock, it may be more difficult to raise or borrow money. Banks are often reluctant to loan money to sole proprietors because of perceived repayment difficulties if the business fails.

Partnership

Definition: A partnership is a company where two or more people share ownership, all contributing money, labor, and skills and sharing the profits of the business. There are three types of partnerships. A *general partnership* assumes that management, liability, and profits are split equally among the partners. Often used for short-term projects, *limited partnerships* permit partners to have limited liability as well as limited input with management decisions. These limits vary according to the extent of each partner's investment percentage. *Joint ventures* are general partnerships, but for only a limited period of time or for a single project. Partners in a joint venture can become an ongoing partnership if they continue the venture, but they must change their agreement and file as a partnership. The terms of any of these partnerships are formulated in a partnership agreement. For a microfarm, a partnership might be one person handling the growing and the other managing value-added products, which are usually processed food products from produce grown in the microfarm.

Formation: Partnerships must register the business with their state, a process usually done through their Secretary of State's office. A business name must be established, usually an assumed name, trade name or a DBA ("doing business as") name. Once the business is registered, the usual licenses and permits must be obtained.

Taxes: Businesses will need to register with the IRS, state and local revenue agencies, and obtain a tax ID number or permit. A partnership must file an "annual information return" to report the income, deductions, gains and losses from the business's operations. Profits or losses are passed through to its partners. Partners include their respective share of the partnership's income or loss on their personal tax returns. Partnership taxes generally include employment taxes. In addition to income tax, partners in the partnership are responsible for self-employment and estimated taxes.

Advantages: Partnerships are usually an inexpensive and easily formed business structure. The most time is spent on developing the partnership agreement. Partnerships have the advantage of pooling resources to obtain capital. This helps with securing credit, or by simply doubling your start-up money. Partnerships also utilize the strengths, resources, and expertise of each partner. Partnerships can have an employment advantage over other entities if they offer employees the opportunity to become a partner.

Disadvantages: In a partnership, partners are not only liable for their own actions, but also for the business debts and decisions made by other partners. With multiple partners, there are bound to be disagreements, so partners should be prepared to consult each other on all decisions, make compromises, and resolve disputes as amicably as possible. Since each partner must share the successes and profits of their business with the other partners, an unequal contribution of time, effort, or resources can cause discord among partners.

Limited Liability Company

Definition: This structure provides some of the limited liability features of a corporation combined with the tax efficiencies and operational advantages of a partnership. The owners of an LLC are referred to as "members," who, depending on state law, might be a single individual (one owner) or two or more individuals, corporations, or other LLCs.

Formation: There are variations state to state, but basically you must choose a name that's different from any other LLC in your state,

that name must have "LLC" tagged on to the end, and it must not have words prohibited by your state, such as "bank" or "insurance," which cannot have this structure. Then, you must file "articles of organization" for your state: a short, simple document that has the business name and address, the names of the members, and the business type and purpose. States vary on the necessity of the members having an operating agreement; this is quite important for any group of people working together. Then you must obtain all necessary permits, and some states require that you publish a statement in the media that announces the creation of your business.

Taxes: Like in a sole proprietorship, profits are passed through to the members in the percentage indicated in the operating agreement, and members add this income onto their personal income taxes. Single member LLCs file a Schedule C, while partners in an LLC file a Form 1065, a partnership tax return, like owners in a typical partnership. An LLC member that is a corporation adds the LLC income when it files Form 1120, the corporation income tax return.

Advantages: Members have limited liability, which means that they don't have personal liability for the company's decisions and debts, but they are not protected from wrongful acts. Compared to an S Corporation, there is less registration paperwork and the start-up costs are less. There are also fewer restrictions on profit sharing within an LLC, as members distribute profits as they like.

Disadvantages: Many states have regulations that result in the dissolution of an LLC if a member leaves it, so the company could have a limited life. And some states allow provisions in the operating agreement to extend the life of an LLC if a member leaves. Also, all individual members of an LLC are considered to be self-employed and must file and pay the self-employment tax contributions towards Medicare and Social Security; the entire net income of the LLC is subject to this tax.

C Corporation

Definition: A C corporation is an independent legal entity owned by shareholders. The corporation itself, not the shareholders that own it, is held legally liable for the actions and debts of the business. Corporations are more complex than other business structures because they have more tax and legal requirements. This structure is usually suggested for established, larger companies with multiple employees. A C corporation offers the ability to sell ownership shares in the business through stock offerings. "Going public" through an initial public offering (IPO) can attract investment capital and high-quality employees.

Formation: A C corporation is formed under the laws of the state in which it is registered.

State laws vary, but generally corporations must include a corporate designation ("Corporation," "Incorporated," or "Limited") at the end of the business name. To register your business as a C corporation, you need to file articles of incorporation with your state's Secretary of State office. Some states require corporations to establish directors and issue stock certificates to initial shareholders during the registration process. Contact your state business entity registration office for precise details about forming a C corporation. Once your business is registered, you must obtain the usual business licenses and permits.

Taxes: C corporations are required to pay federal, state, and in some cases, local taxes because they are separate tax-paying entities. Regular corporations are called "C corporations" because Subchapter C of Chapter 1 of the Internal Revenue Code is where you find general tax rules affecting corporations and their shareholders. Unlike sole proprietors and partnerships, C corporations pay income tax on their profits. C corporations use IRS Form 1120 or 1120-A, U.S. Corporation Income Tax Return, to report revenue to the federal government. The

Pets cannot be legal partners in a corporation, sorry.
Photo by Dwight Sipler.

corporation and the employee each pay one half of the Social Security and Medicare taxes, but this is usually a deductible business expense.

Advantages: With a C corporation, shareholders' personal assets are protected from the debts and liabilities of the company. Shareholders can generally only be held accountable for their investment in stock of the company. C corporations have the ability to raise funds through the sale of stock. Owners of a C corporation only pay taxes on corporate profits paid to them in the form of salaries, bonuses, and dividends, while any additional profits are awarded a corporate tax rate, which is usually lower than a personal income tax rate. C corporations can offer employees partial ownership through stock options and thus attract high-quality workers.

Disadvantages: A C corporation is a more costly and time-consuming structure to use than the other options. Incorporation requires start-up, operating, and tax costs that most other structures do not require. Because C corporations are highly regulated by federal, state, and in some cases local agencies, there are increased paperwork and recordkeeping requirements associated with this business structure. And C corporation owners are usually taxed twice: once when the C corporation makes a profit, and again when dividends are paid to shareholders.

S Corporation

Definition: What makes an S corporation different from a C corporation is that profits and losses can pass through to your personal tax return. The business itself is not taxed—only the shareholders are taxed. The shareholders must be paid fair market value, or the IRS might reclassify any additional corporate earnings as "wages." For shareholders, liability protection is limited. S corporations do not necessarily shield you from all litigation, such as an employee's lawsuit as a result of a workplace incident.

Formation: To file as an S corporation, you must first file as a C corporation. After you are considered a corporation, all shareholders must sign and file Form 2553 to elect your corporation to become an S corporation. Once your business is registered, you must obtain the usual business licenses and permits. You can request S corporation status for your LLC. Your attorney can advise you on the pros and cons of doing this. You'll have to make a special election with the IRS to have the LLC taxed as an S corporation using Form 2553, filing it before the first two months and fifteen days of the beginning of the tax year in which the election is to take effect. The LLC remains a limited liability company from a legal standpoint, but for tax purposes it's treated as an S corporation.

Taxes: States do not tax S corporations equally. Most recognize them similarly to the federal government and tax the shareholders accordingly, but some states (like Massachusetts) tax S corporations on profits above a specified limit. Other states don't recognize the S corporation election and treat the business as a C corporation with that tax structure. Some states (like New York and New Jersey) tax both the S corporation's profits and the shareholder's proportional shares of the profits.

Advantages: While members of an LLC are subject to employment tax on the entire net income of the business, only the wages of the S corporation shareholder who is an employee are subject to employment tax. The remaining income is paid to the owner as a "distribution," which is taxed at a lower rate, if at all. An S corporation designation allows a business to have an independent life, separate from its shareholders. If a shareholder leaves the company, or sells his or her shares, the S corporation can continue doing business relatively undisturbed.

Disadvantages: S corporations require scheduled director and shareholder meetings, minutes from those meetings, adoption and updates to bylaws, stock transfers, and records maintenance. A shareholder must receive reasonable compensation. The IRS takes notice of shareholder red flags like low salary/high distribution combinations, and may reclassify your distributions as wages.

Cooperatives

Definition: This structure is a business or organization owned by and operated for the benefit of those using its services. All profits and earnings generated by the cooperative are distributed among the members, also known as user-owners. Usually, an elected board of directors and officers operates the cooperative while regular members have voting power to control the direction of the cooperative. This is one of the more complicated business structures and anyone reading this book to start a microfarm is unlikely to use it, so I'm not going to explain it in more detail here. You should consult a business attorney if you are interested in this option.

What's in a Name?

The naming of my microfarm was accidental. After I decided to use five-gallon pots for many of my superhot chile plants, I realized that I would need a soil expander, namely perlite, a naturally-occurring amorphous volcanic glass that when heated turns into very light, inert granules that prevent soil-packing in containers. And I needed a lot of it, but the product is expensive in the small bags sold by the big box home centers. I decided that I needed an account at a wholesale supplier. When I opened one, I thought of the name "Sunbelt Microfarm" on the spot.

The first step in establishing your brand is to give it a name. Hopefully, you will spend longer thinking about it than I did, because your identity—what other people call you—is more important than you think. Face it, "Dave's Farm" is not an imaginative name at all, nor is "DeWitt's Farm." They both sound too small and a little amateurish. You want a farm name that sounds substantial and a little impersonal, but memorable. There's a small farm here in the South Valley called "Red Tractor Farm," and I like the whimsical nature of the name. I thought about changing the name of mine to "No Tractor Farm," but I didn't want anyone to think that I was using a mule and a plow.

Since you have to plan ahead, even from the very beginning, you should think about what you might call some value-added products. Does Sunbelt Microfarm's Pickled Superhot Chiles have a ring to it? Sort of, but if someone's not already using it, Sunbelt Pickled Superhot Chiles is stronger and better. It is also possible to have an overall company name, and then a different brand name or names for your products. For example, an exhibitor in our National

Fiery Foods & Barbecue Show, Apple Canyon Gourmet, has differently named brands because they bought several failing companies and turned them around. They didn't want to rename the products because they were already branded.

And you want to avoid triteness. Because the Sandia Mountains hover over the city of Albuquerque, there are many, many businesses with the name "Sandia" in them. So many, in fact, it's become both trite and absurd, once you understand what "sandia" means in Spanish. Near sunset, the low sun in the west causes the west-facing slopes to have a distinct reddish tint that is exactly the color of the flesh of a watermelon, and that's precisely what "sandia" means. The translation reveals the absurdity of calling your business the "Watermelon Mental Health Clinic." Likewise for "Watermelon Dog Obedience Club," or "Watermelon Crust Pizza Company," which is a pun on the highest point of the Sandias, Sandia Crest. Often, regionalism is confusing and is not a good thing.

My mentor, the late, great Frank Crosby, was a show producer too and would never in a million years have called his business "Sandia Entertainment Company"—he had a much larger vision than that. He named it the Entertainment Corporation of America. Before you say that the name is a bit grandiose for a small Albuquerque company, I should point out that Frank had once been a standup vaudeville comedian who always told jokes like, "Did you hear the one about the farmer's daughter who sits among the beans and peas?"

My point here is to think big. If your microfarm is in the Midwest, I plead with you *not* to call it "Little Microfarm on the Prairie." It's clever, but make it a brand for your products rather than your company name. Likewise for

"Pacific," "Rockies," "Bayou," and so on. Think more symbolically than locally—that's why I chose Sunbelt Shows, Inc. for my corporate name. It says what the company does primarily but is deliberately vague as to regional location, allowing for easy expansion into other markets, which we did successfully for a while with food shows.

The Small Business Administration has some good advice about choosing a name for your business. Don't get lazy and just name the business with your family name because that makes it more difficult to present a professional image and build brand awareness. You must consider how your name will look as part of a logo, on a website, and in social media. Does the name directly reflect what business the company is in, and most importantly, is it unique? You should select a name that has not been used by others, either online or offline. There are several ways to check the name you've selected: a simple web search, a trademark search through the U.S. Patent and Trademark website (Uspto.gov), a domain name search through the WHOSIS database (NetworkSolutions.com), and through your state filing office. Registering your "Doing Business As" name is simply the process of letting your state government know that you are doing business as a name other than your personal name or the legal name of your partnership or corporation. If you are operating under your own name, then you can skip the process.

Value-Added Products: How to Manufacture and Market Them

The first thing you should do if you're interested in this type of expansion is to buy a copy of *From Kitchen to Market: Selling Your*

Gourmet Food Specialty, by Stephen Hall. It is the most comprehensive book on the subject and will probably lead you to making the right decision. Of course, Hall wrote an entire book on this, so I can't include all of it here. But since I've been producing a show for these types of products for the last twenty-five years, I know a lot about this subject, so I can give you the highlights of what to expect.

What type of product(s) should you make? The most obvious ones to me are concentrates of what you're currently growing, assuming that's possible. This is why I've turned my ripe tomatoes into purees and sun-dried slices. This is basic "manufacturing" and as long as you're selling to chefs and not to the general public, usually you won't need a particular license or even a manufacturing facility. Make sure you check your state's regulations on this issue. Assuming you have some basic equipment, concentrated forms of your products will be simple to make and will require freezing or drying after they are processed. After the basics, there are an astounding number of products that can be made, and research into the specialty food market will be required. One of the simplest ways to learn a lot about the different products out there is to go to a trade show where they are on display. The Fancy Foods Shows, produced by the Specialty Food Association, are a good place to start, as is my show, the National Fiery Foods & Barbecue Show.

Who will buy them? Generally speaking, your first customers will be your farm customers who already know and trust your unprocessed farm products. The next wave of customers will come from your contacts at farmers' markets, so be sure that you have your new products well-displayed and even offer them for tasting. From there, you want your products continually on display locally at specialty food stores and even supermarkets. After that, I suggest (of course), exhibiting in food shows as your first form of advertising beyond the basics explained earlier.

Where are they made? Most states do not allow food made in home kitchens to be sold to the general public, with the possible exception of baked goods like cookies, pies, and cakes sold at nonprofit bake sales. This means you need to use a commercial kitchen if you want to produce and pack the products, or find a contract packer (called a co-packer) to do it for you. (The best way to find a co-packer is to ask manufacturers of non-competing products who packs theirs.) I think that usually you should go with the latter option because how much can you do? You're a farmer, a food producer, and a marketer all at the same time? You're going to need employees, and that is very expensive. Better to let someone else worry about paying the help needed to pack products. Yes, there are often problems with co-packers changing recipes to cut expenses, or using cheaper containers, but you can monitor all this in a lot less time than spending all day on your feet packing food into jars. And don't even *think* about building your own commercial kitchen. How many headaches do you need?

What kind of packaging is right for the products? Some are easy. Your microfarm grows seventeen different kinds of mustard seed, and you're going to make packaged gourmet mustard. Have you seen it packaged in anything other than glass jars, plastic squeeze bottles, or tiny plastic single-serve pouches? But some ingredients, like chile peppers, have a myriad of packaging possibilities. Today, for example, I discovered a squeeze tube of chipotle pepper paste. Who woulda thought? Again, attend a gourmet products trade show and speak with some product packaging companies. Since they want your business, they will give you plenty of free advice that should all be taken, as the Roman cooks used to say, *cum grano salis* (look it up).

How will you store and ship these products? No, your greenhouse can't be your warehouse. It would be wonderful if you just moved your products from the co-packer to a food distributor's warehouse, but that's not going to happen for a while. So you will have to play it by ear and move slowly as you learn the business. Now is the time to consider mail-order sales, whether you might need a delivery truck or van, and how far away you want your products distributed if you have to do it yourself. All of this begs two questions....

How will you distribute them? And, **How will you market and advertise them?** You need to pick some people's brains. Find the owner of a company that has products that will not compete with yours, get to know him or her, buy them some coffee or a drink, and start brainstorming. Find out what they do with their products and keep two lists—one of ideas you like, and one of ideas you don't. Talk with some managers of local markets and ask them about their most popular locally made products, and what makes them sell. Discuss the situation with your co-packer, if you have one, and get some advice. At food shows, casually ask exhibitors (at slow times) how they advertise and if they have a distributor they could recommend. You're researching, assembling the data you will need to plan a direction to take, a strategy.

I wish I could be more specific here, but there are hundreds and hundreds of specialty food products, each one with its own wants and needs. There are just too many variables to give

more detailed directions about marketing specific products, or even product categories. Besides, you need to do this anyway. It's part of your microfarm education.

Other Ideas for Your Microfarm, Some Crazy

Agritourism rules! Since my wife and I can never enjoy a normal vacation, like lying on the beach reading trashy novels, or seeing all the cathedrals in Spain, we have essentially become agritourists. In that capacity, we have visited fascinating agriculturally related places all over the world. I mention these to give potential microfarmers ideas of how they might exploit the agritourism aspects of their farm. As the Small Farm Center at the University of California notes, "Agricultural tourism or agritourism, is one alternative for improving the incomes and potential economic viability of small farms and rural communities." We shopped for Scotch bonnet peppers in the produce markets of Ocho Rios, Jamaica, then snuck into the ganja fields, and we kept our balance when we visited the steeply sloped herb fields of Paramin, Trinidad, and then examined a Congo pepper plantation with ganja fields next door. (The agricultural Caribbean is like that!) And of course, we went to the Royal Botanic Garden in Port of Spain, and the Botanic Station in Tobago, where the first superhot chiles probably originated. We bought bags of peppercorns at a black pepper plantation in Costa Rica and visited the rain-soaked red habanero fields of the aptly-named town of Los Chiles.

In Italy, after visiting the Olive Oil Museum near Lake Garda, we stayed in an *agriturismo* stone house in the middle of a vineyard, visited an olive-pressing factory, a grappa-making plant, the largest ornamental chile field in the world, and met a pack of truffle-hunting puppies on a farm outside of Parma. We also stayed on a microfarm near Bardi in Emilia Romagna, owned and managed by Maurizio Bovi and Luisa Sgarbossa. The couple purchased and remodeled an old rock-built farmhouse named Ca'd'Alfieri that they run as a bed and breakfast and also a restaurant for the guests. They grow fruit and vegetables that they sell at markets around northern Italy, raise farm animals including black pigs, and live off the land they own and work. In Germany, we visited numerous breweries of varying sizes, and sticking with beer, visited a hop processing plant and museum.

In Mexico, we cooked *mole* sauce in the middle of a farm of chile plants grown only in Oaxaca, shopped in numerous outdoor markets including Mexico City's enormous La Merced, the largest retail traditional food market in the city of nine million people. We went out to catch *hamachi* (yellowtail) with the local fishermen in Baja in a *ponga* boat (that's called harvesting from nature), and visited with a tilapia and neem tree farmer in Yucatán. On another trip to Yucatán, we visited the habanero chile fields, sorting and processing plants, and the laboratories devoted to that crop in Mérida.

On our culinary tour of India, led by England's King of Curries, Pat Chapman, we watched *paneer* cheese being made in the open kitchen at the Shikarbadi Hunting Lodge in Udaipur, took cooking lessons, and enjoyed the meals that were specially prepared for us by the head chefs of the Taj Hotel Group. Singapore was market after market, each representative of the major population groups of the country: Chinese, Malay, and Indian. No, there was not a British market. We took cooking classes, had a drink at Raffles Hotel, and ate fish-head soup.

Michael Coelho and Dave DeWitt in the Herb Fields of Paramin, 1992. Photo by Mary Jane Wilan.

The Chile Pepper Institute's teaching and demonstration garden at New Mexico State University. Photo courtesy of NMSU.

In Johor Bahru, Malaysia, we shopped in a mall supermarket and discovered two forty-foot aisles of racks eight feet high filled only with chile sauces and pastes. Some of the best spicy food we ate in Asia was in Thailand, so we had to go to the wholesale market and see their gigantic display of chile peppers packed every way you can imagine. A vendor warned me in sign language not to eat a tiny *prik kee nu* chile but I just grinned and popped it in my mouth. The vendor just shook her head in amazement that a *farangi* could actually eat one.

The United States offered us many agritourism delights like the largest produce show in the country in New Orleans, and I marveled at the weird warehouse of Melissa's, the specialty produce company near L.A. in California, where

I could only identify twenty percent of the fruits and vegetables I saw. In the Texas Hill Country, I went on a feral hog hunt and helped smoke some of the delicious pork we, ahem, harvested. We have dropped in on chile farms all over the country, and I did a demonstration on cooking with curries at the Scottsdale Culinary Festival before a crowd of eight hundred in a theater.

And, of course, we have visited a few cactus and succulent microfarms and they were every bit as interesting as botanical gardens, which is precisely what they were—with the exception that every display was for sale. The Demonstration Garden of the Chile Pepper Institute, on the campus of New Mexico State University in Las Cruces, gets hundreds—if not thousands—of visitors during the growing season every year who want to see what 150 varieties in the same field look like. There's no way to count the number of visitors because the field is in the open near Main Street with no fences, and when the pods are ripe, anyone can harvest them. Imagine a field like that as part of your "you pick 'em" microfarm with, of course, a little more security and a cash register.

Now I will reveal five microfarm ideas with both value-added products and agritourism appeal. As far as I know, none of these really exist, but they could. Some would require a sizable capital investment; others, long hours and weekend work; and one, additional liability insurance. Now, can I write a coherent microplan for each of them? We'll see.

The Mushroom Grotto and Pâté Factory. Not too many microfarms will have a natural cave on the premises, so you would have to build one like those winding "underground" zoo displays, or the museum designs that take you through the exhibits until you end up in the museum store. Of course, as a mushroom professional, you would not actually be growing them in the displays, but rather in separate, special houses that also could be visited by guests and customers.

It would probably be considered insensitive to hire children dressed like elves to work in the grotto, but I couldn't resist mentioning the idea. Promotions to draw customers would obviously include Halloween, but don't forget about Walpurgis Night, a traditional spring festival in central Europe on April 30 or May 1, exactly six months away from Halloween. Legend holds that mushroom fairy rings mark the spots where witches were dancing on that night. You could have a mid-summer mushroom festival modeled after the Telluride, Colorado Shroomfest, now in its thirty-third year. Activities could include mycologists giving mushroom and toadstool identification clinics, a mushroom cook-off contest, hands-on growing workshops, showings of mushroom movies like *Shrooms* (horror), *Know Your Mushrooms* (documentary), *Attack of the Mushroom People* (horror), or *Now Forager* (drama).

Value-added products for the Grotto Gift Shop include mushroom supplements and nutraceuticals for health, and edible mushroom-growing kits for morels, shiitakes, and oysters. Also, you could sell dried and fresh mushrooms, plug spawn, truffle oils, pâtés, herbal teas, books, and posters. There are dozens and dozens of mushroom-related gifts and accessories, including clothing, candles, art and sculptures, jewelry, magnets, and even lamps.

The Edible Aquarium and Sushi Bar. Everyone's seen the live lobsters in tanks in the supermarkets, and Asian markets often have large aquariums with live fish swimming around in them. This idea for a microfarm expands those concepts and the choices for the consumer for the freshest seafood possible. If some microfarms are "you pick," this one could be "you catch," so that your customers could enjoy a fishing experience as well as a shopping one. It's a good idea for attracting families with kids. There's no charge for catch and release, but if they want to take the catch home for eating, they pay by the pound.

Admittedly, aquaculture has its technical challenges, but it is the "wave" of the future. Here are some of the methods used.

—Open-net pens or cages enclose fish such as salmon in offshore coastal areas or in freshwater lakes. Note that this practice is regarded as environmentally destructive.

—Ponds hold fish in a coastal or inland body of fresh or salt water. Shrimp, catfish, and tilapia are commonly farmed in this manner.

—Raceways divert water from a stream or well, so that it flows through channels containing the fish. In the U.S., farmers use raceways to raise rainbow trout.

—Recirculating systems in tanks treat and recirculate the water to keep the fish healthy. Tanks can be used to farm such species as striped bass, salmon, and sturgeon.

—Shellfish culture is a method farmers use to grow shellfish on beaches or suspend them in the water by ropes, plastic trays, or mesh bags. The most commonly raised shellfish are oysters, mussels, and clams.

A seafood restaurant with a sushi bar could be part of the microfarm, making it an even more popular destination, but of course not everyone wants to be a restaurateur. The Rappahannock Oyster Company has three such restaurants in Virginia, and their oyster farm provides the basis for them. Instead of value-added products, the aquaculture microfarm would have a gift shop with seafood related merchandise including cookbooks, seafood cooking tools and supplies, and fresh seafood for sale.

I would recommend that anyone attempting such a microfarm take university courses in aquaculture. Some universities offering them are Auburn, the University of California-Davis, Hawaii, Louisiana State, Maryland, Cornell, South Carolina, and quite a few more.

The Beautiful But Deadly Microfarm and Poison Museum. This microfarm would grow and sell beautiful, ornamental, and poisonous—but legal—plants. Nathaniel Hawthorne wrote about just such a microfarm in 1844: "Nothing could exceed the intentness with which this scientific gardener examined every shrub which grew in his path.... The man's demeanor was that of one walking among malignant influences,

Poisonous plants like deadly nightshade (*Datura wrightii*) would be growing in the The Beautiful But Deadly Microfarm and Poison Museum. NPS Photo by Neal Herbert.

such as savage beasts, or deadly snakes, or evil spirits, which should he allow them one moment of license, would wreak upon him some terrible fatality." Hawthorne was way ahead of his time in his portrayal of Dr. Rappaccini's poisonous garden. There are now similar gardens around the world, including the Alnwick Poison Garden in Northumberland, England, the poison section of the Botanical Garden of Padua, the Chelsea Physic Garden in London, the Toxic Plant Garden within the Montreal Botanical Garden, the Medicinal Garden at the Mütter Museum in Philadelphia, and the W.C. Muenscher Poisonous Plants Garden at Cornell University. There are also drug plant gardens in various locations. The Maynard W. Quimby Medicinal Plant Garden at the University of Mississippi has what it calls the "correctly identified living plant collection" that grows about 1,500 species from all geographic regions of the world. Another drug garden is under development at the University of South Florida.

Many people are unaware that some of the more beautiful ornamental landscaping plants are poisonous. Here are just a few examples of the plants in this microfarm.

—Datura or jimsonweed, with its large and beautiful flowers, has a long history of use both in South America and Europe and is known for causing delirious states and poisonings in uninformed users. Most parts of the plant contain atropine, scopolamine, and hyoscyamine.

—Henbane is a biennial herb that grows up to one meter tall and produces spectacular veined yellow flowers and large quantities of seeds. It was historically used in combination with mandrake, deadly nightshade, and datura as an anesthetic potion, as well as for its psychoactive properties in "magic brews."

—Oleander, a common landscaping plant with beautiful flowers of many colors, is extremely poisonous. Every part of the plant affects the heart, produces severe digestive upset, and has caused death.

—Deadly Nightshade, or belladonna, is a one- to two-meter tall perennial herb that produces small red to black berries from bright purple flowers. These berries contain atropine, scopolamine, and hyoscyamine and have a long history of use as a medicinal, poisonous, and ceremonial herb.

Others include castor bean, lantana, lily of the valley, lupine, mistletoe, philodendron, azalea, Boston and English ivy, clematis, holly, hydrangea, sago palm, Virginia creeper, and wisteria. The microfarm would sell seeds, bedding plants, large specimen plants, books like Mark Mills' *The Savage Garden*, Albert Hofmann and Richard Evans Schultes' *Plants of the Gods*, and Amy Stewart's *Wicked Plants*. Special promotions could include seminars on protecting your pets and farm animals from poisonous houseplants, garden plants, and weeds, and talks on drug plants. I would imagine that Halloween with a witches' brew of plants that cause spells would be a big hit. The possibilities for promotions on local, regional, and national media would generate a lot of traffic to this microfarm because people are fascinated by deadly things—and especially the ones that seem so innocent.

The Gourdgeous Garden and Squash Courts. Gourds might seem an unlikely crop for a microfarm, but I think a cucurbit enthusiast could make go of it with gourds and squashes because they are so versatile. Gourds can be your dinner or the serving bowl for it, the dipping spoon for your squash soup, your vegetable sponge, your birdhouses, your works of art, your vases, your fishing bobber, your herb planter, your weird wall hangings, and even your banjo, rattle, flute, marimbas, or drums. And when I write "squash courts," I'm not kidding: both gourds and squashes will grow vertically, so theoretically, with the right structure and some netting, you could give the illusion of a squash or racquetball court. Google around for "chayote" and note that to save ground space, they usually hang from netting and trellises.

For promotions to attract customers, a gourd art show and competition would be a lot of fun. After all, some of the most gorgeous painted gourds are the *jícaras* from Mexico and Guatemala. And gourd carving is a celebrated art in Nigeria and New Zealand. What about a concert featuring the Berry Gourdy String Band, with all the musicians playing with gourd-only instruments? For value-added products, what about bottled winter squash pasta sauces? I've tried some splendid ones. You could even serve them over spaghetti squash. There are canned acorn or butternut squash soups, and squash flour is popular for baking in the Philippines.

Worried about squash bugs? Hint: keep chickens or guinea fowl for eggs or meat and give them access to the squash garden for an hour each day and soon you won't have any bugs—or grasshoppers for that matter.

The Popcorn Crazy Farm and Family Fun Maze. This would fit into the category of agritainment. There are plenty of corn mazes around the country, but I've never heard of one tied into popcorn. There is some method to my madness because popcorn is a profitable value-added product, especially if you're growing your own.

Corn mazes usually have some value-added entertainment in addition to the maze. These include hay rides, zip lines, live zombie scarecrows or other Halloween figures, corn cannons, which can shoot an ear of corn quite a ways, elaborate children's playgrounds, a live pumpkin princess, and a you-pick pumpkin patch. Some have pig races, a petting zoo, play areas for children, and picnic areas. Some are open after dark for Flashlight Nights. Admission to all entertainment events is usually between $8.00 and $20.00.

The elaborately designed mazes used to be hacked out of a main field using machetes, and that was exhausting work. Now farmers

A corn maze in Delinsdorf, Germany.
Photo by Karsten H. Eggert.

have wised up and use spatial management computer software to fashion the designs. When the corn is about two feet tall, the maze design is transferred to the cornfield using global positioning technology. The corn is then mowed or tilled under, but some farmers use herbicides to kill the corn plants for paths wide enough to accommodate wheelchairs and strollers.

Maze operators develop yearly themes for their mazes, like Wild West, Egyptian, or political candidates, and they can tie quizzes into the themes. Of course the maze themes can only be viewed from the air, but customers are usually given a map so they can guide themselves around. There are usually Maze Masters to help people around the maze so we don't read headlines like "Five South Korean Tourists Go Missing in Hilary Clinton Corn Maze; Helicopters Called In." Think that's just my imagination running rampant? Well, the Adventure Acres corn maze in Bellbrook, Ohio, just outside of Dayton, consists of sixty-two acres of corn maze with over eight miles of trails!

Value-added products for sale at the maze could include flavored popcorns (cheddar, caramel, chocolate, brown sugar and cinnamon, coconut, toffee, curry cashew, red chile—the list is very long), and custom popcorn boxes and bags with your microfarm name and logo on them.

Since this microfarm will be both agritourism and agritainment, you should have the usual souvenirs for sale (they double as promotional items): popcorn maze postcards, aerial photos, stickers, coasters, caps, t-shirts, mugs, and whatever else crazy you can think up.

Brett Herbst is probably the king of corn mazes; he began designing them in 1996 and now has his own maze design and consultation business. "People don't pay to walk through a corn maze," he says. "People are paying for a memorable experience. No one ever comes to a corn maze alone." When you're with a group, "You have to make all these decisions together and you know that everybody is going to be wrong at some point in time going through the maze. That's what relationships are built on—sharing ideas and thoughts and challenging one another."

Of course, these are just fantasies until someone takes an idea and runs with it. I've written these with a bit of whimsy, but I think a microfarmer should have a good sense of humor. Perhaps one of these ideas will inspire a future microfarmer to come up with a truly imaginative—and profitable—farming operation. If you do that, you'd better learn how to sell what you produce.

Possible Microfarming Plants and Animals

I use the word "possible" here rather than "recommended" because each microfarmer must decide personally which crops best fit his or her plan. I chose these particular crops because their higher value and growing habits make them suitable for smaller farming operations. It doesn't make much sense to grow field crops or grain crops on a microfarm because their value depends on greater production than a microfarmer could ever accomplish. The crops are in alphabetical order.

About the Crop

Baby ginger is precisely what its name implies: immature rhizomes that lack the tough skin and potent pungency of store-bought mature ginger. It does not require peeling and does not have a fibrous center, so cooks can simply chop it and use it. Baby ginger as a culinary ingredient is unfamiliar to most consumers and even chefs, so let them know in advance about your coming crop to get them interested in future purchases. During harvest time, it's important to educate the public on using and storing the baby ginger that they purchase, so you should create an information sheet with basic uses and a couple of recipes.

Ginger is part of the genus Zingiber, which has about a hundred species of perennial plants, many of which are grown as ornamentals. The different species of Zingiber have many culinary uses—for example, the shoots and flowers of *Zingiber mioga*, the Japanese ginger, are used fresh or pickled as a flavoring in Japanese cuisine, such as the familiar accompaniment to sushi and sashimi.

The principal cultivated ginger is *Zingiber officinale*, native to tropical Asia, which is a deciduous perennial with thick, branching rhizomes, upright stems, and long, pointed leaves. The flowers are quite lovely—yellow-green with purple and yellow lips. The plant can grow up to four feet tall. The flavor and heat levels vary greatly, as Australian spice expert Ian Hemphill notes: "The flavour will be similarly tangy, sweet, spicy and warm to hot, depending upon when it has been harvested, as to a large degree early harvested [baby] ginger is sweet and tender, while later harvested rhizomes are more fibrous and pungent."

The volatile oils causing the pungency are gingerols and shogaols. The shogaols appear when ginger is dried and they are much more pungent, so dried ginger is hotter than fresh. It also has less water, so the pungency is more concentrated. Gingerol is commonly used to treat poor digestion, heartburn, and motion sickness.

Baby ginger.
Photo courtesy of Sunbelt Archives.

Pros

Basically, for ginger, the pros are the value-added products that come from the crop. There are two methods of processing ginger to make value-added products. One is to preserve it in brine, syrup, or in crystallized form. The other is to dry it and then, optionally, to grind it into powder.

Pickled ginger is made from fresh rhizomes that are sliced as thin as paper, then placed in a vinegar solution. The acetic acid in the vinegar turns the ginger pink. In Japan, pickled ginger is known as *gari* and it is considered a palate refresher between courses, and it is commonly served with sushi and sashimi.

Dried ginger is made from the more mature rhizomes, which are peeled by the farmers and left to dry in the sun, which is not the cleanest method. Increasingly, more ginger is being furnace-dried. After drying, the rhizomes are ground into powder and bottled.

Cons

The plants require not only a long growing period (which, on a farm, especially a microfarm, can easily monopolize valuable real estate) but also ample amounts of water and just the right soil temperature. Baby ginger is fussy and it likes constant warmth but not excessive heat. The plant generally requires soil between fifty and ninety degrees, which essentially means that the east coast states are not the best place to grow it unless you use a greenhouse, tunnels, or hoop houses. The late winter and early spring months are too cold, and the summers are much too hot. It is possible to grow baby ginger in containers, but the yields are too small to make this practical.

The storage time after harvest is much shorter for baby ginger than it is for mature ginger, which can often last for months in the store or your refrigerator. Baby ginger can be stored at room temperature for only about two to three weeks after harvest. This limits the market season, but also means that competition for the crop is small and it cannot be shipped from overseas producers. Ginger is one of the most fragile of all the spicy ingredients because its heat fades so quickly, especially after processing and when cooked.

Baby ginger is becoming so popular as a specialty crop that the main seed suppliers, like East Branch Ginger and its parent, Puna Organics, often sell out of seeds. And if you save your own for replanting, you risk diseases like fusarium and bacterial wilt.

Bottom Line

Selling for up to $15 a pound, depending upon inventory, competition, and farm location, even slow-growing baby ginger can defeat some of the cons with its high price. To reduce the price shock for customers, it is best to pick a per-pound price and break the baby ginger into smaller pieces to sell by the ounce. In addition to selling baby ginger as whole or sectioned rhizomes, you can also market a number of value-added products, mentioned above. Just remember one thing, though: the only state with a commercial ginger crop is Hawaii, so if you live elsewhere, most of your farming effort will go into climate modification to make the plant happy and producing well in your microfarm.

About the Crop

First, you need to establish your bee colony where there's a lot of flowering plants. Suburban and rural land make the best options, although there are urban beekeepers. Then you need a hive of bees, complete with a live queen. You might be able to buy an established hive from another beekeeper, which is a good way to start, but only buy a colony that's been inspected either by an apiarist from your state department of agriculture (that's usually a free service) or by someone you know who knows bees. But the most common and reliable way of starting out is to simply order your bees by mail. A package colony will devote most of its energy during its first season to building up the number of bees and food for the winter, so you probably won't get your own honey harvest from it until the second year. Where do you put colonies? Many urban beekeepers put their hives on their rooftops, out of the way of pedestrians. People with hives in crowded neighborhoods keep them out of sight, preferably behind a bush or barrier so the insects will have to fly up a few feet to head out foraging. Raising bees for honey is tricky, so don't be self-reliant. Contact your local beekeeping society (your county extension agent can put you in touch) and find out the name of a competent hobby beekeeper who'd be willing to show you around his or her backyard apiary and give you instruction and advice.

A honeybee on a modern hive in an apiary.
Photo by Björn Appel.

Pros

My favorite beekeeping quote is by "Kenpkr" on an online forum: "There is no other field of animal husbandry like beekeeping. It has the appeal to the scientist, the nature lover, and even (or especially) the philosopher. It is a chance to work with some of the most fascinating of God's creatures, to spend time and do work in the great outdoors, to challenge my abilities and continue to learn. My hope is that I never become so frail with old age that I cannot spend my days among the bees. It gives credence to the old saying that 'the best things in life are free.'"

Of course, you're in it for the honey, and the amount you harvest will depend on how many hives you have and how many flowering plants there are in a mile or so radius from your hives. If you package and sell your honey, you need to

have a unique selling proposition, like a particular nectar that the bees collect, such as lavender. The most unique angle I've heard of came from Reed Booth in Bisbee, Arizona, who is a killer bee removal expert featured in Part 2. His honey, of course, is Killer Bee Honey, and some has chile powder in it. Wax is another popular product of bees, and the bees store the honey in wax combs. Wax is used in many products, including candles, creams, and cosmetics. You could make your own lip balm as a value-added product. And the rest of your microfarm will benefit because pollination is what bees do, and if you want healthy plants, bees can help. Many cities have legalized beekeeping, with New York joining Chicago, Detroit, Cleveland, Minneapolis, Atlanta, and San Francisco in approving urban hives. Beekeepers must adhere to published guidelines, which might include lot size, cleanliness, provision of water, and advice on managing the honey bee colony's natural swarming instinct.

Cons

Stings can be a major drawback for the would-be beekeeper. Check with your doctor first to find out if you have a hypoallergenic reaction to bee stings. Even if you are not allergic, stings can still be painful. Fortunately, most beekeepers develop immunity to the poison over time. Supplies can get expensive because you will have to invest in a hive, proper clothing, a smoker, extracting equipment, and hive supplies. Prices vary, but a single new hive may cost about $110, clothing and gear may cost about $160, and a package of new bees may run $75 to $100. Often you can find starter kits with bees, boxes, and gear for a better combined price. A lot of people lose bees because farmers or gardeners

spray the flowers of crops that bees work. You might have to educate your neighbors about safe spraying and warn them not to use Sevin. There are a few honey bee diseases, the worst of which is American foulbrood. By law, you have to destroy infested colonies to keep the disease from infecting other hives. One of the biggest threats to honey bees is the varroa mite—the parasite lays its eggs in the hives and feeds on the bees during the winter. And a number of colonies starve each winter, primarily because their owners didn't leave enough honey in the hive to last until the following spring flowers arrive, usually in April. Bee colony collapse disorder, which has received much media attention, mostly affects the bees in colonies that are moved around the U.S. to pollinate certain crops like almonds.

Bottom Line

If you're in a good beekeeping area, and if the weather's excellent that year, you could possibly get thirty to sixty gallons from a single hive, but that would be very unusual. Count on about fifteen to twenty gallons as a more reasonable single-hive harvest. A sixteen-ounce jar of raw honey retails for about $15, so you may have to invest in several hives to make significant profits. Consider speaking with other microfarmers and work deals to place your hives near their crops, like lavender, alfalfa, or raspberries, so that you can make a varietal honey that will be worth more. Usually, you will share the harvest with the landowner. Other value-added products with honey are honey butters, honey mustards, honey cookies or other sweets, including baklava. Don't forget to have a consistent brand for your honey and products, including candles and other products made from beeswax.

About the Crop

Although raising chickens for eggs has a nice cachet, and there are magazines and blogs devoted to urban chicken care, you would have to have a fairly large flock and a good egg marketing plan to have a microfarm based solely around chickens. Chickens are better as part of an overall diversified microfarm, such as a small dairy operation where eggs joined the other dairy products produced, like cheeses, yogurt, or ice cream. Because chickens are such excellent egg producers—each hen lays about three hundred eggs per year—your egg supply can have many uses. They can be ingredients in baked products, can be bartered for other foods that you're currently not growing, and with proper permitting, sold along with your other microfarm crops at stands or farmers' markets.

Pros

Raising your own microfarm flock will give you free garden fertilizer, natural insect control in your yard (they *love* grasshoppers and crickets) and growing areas (although chickens do eat vegetables), fresh eggs that are free from added chemicals, and when the hens are through laying in a few years, you'll have them for the cooking pot. Caring for chickens is easier than most other pets and without a rooster in the mix, they are relatively quiet and make good household pets.

Domestic free range chickens should be part of a varied microfarm. Photo by Aleks.

Cons

Chickens require a hen house to sleep in and lay eggs in, so you'll have to build one or buy one. They need fresh water every day, proper bedding, and good food. They must be babied and kept quite warm until they get all their feathers, protected from all predators including the family dog and cat, and are subject to quite a few diseases and occasionally lice. You can be pecked occasionally because some chickens are ill-tempered. My friend who raises chickens (I trade her culinary herbs for eggs) had a rooster that was so mean that she had him killed and taxidermied, and he now occupies a spot of honor in her living room. And finally, chickens are messy.

Bottom Line

A small flock of chickens around your microfarm is charming and often amusing, especially if they fit into your overall plan for a microfarm. A flock of six hens will produce about 1,800 eggs per year, and that's 150 dozen. If you sold a dozen in a carton for $3.00, your gross income would only be $450, and you would have to pay for the feed and other expenses. However, if your microfarm had other uses for the eggs, they could be transformed into more value-added products. Your challenge, if you want chickens, is to formulate that plan to incorporate them conveniently into your microfarm and not plan an entire microfarm around them.

About the Crop

Chile peppers, like tomatoes, are fruits of the large Solanaceae or nightshade family, which also includes potatoes, tobacco, tomatillos, petunias, and the poisonous mandrake, belladonna, and datura, or jimsonweed. Chiles have their own "poison," namely their active ingredient, capsaicin, which seems to have evolved to protect the seeds from consumption by mammals, whose digestive systems destroy their seeds. As a spice, chiles are second in popularity only to black pepper, and as a food, they heat up cuisines all around the world, from Mexico to India to Hungary to Thailand to China. In fact, India is the number one producer of dried chiles and China the leader in the cultivation of fresh ones. Fresh chiles of some sort are commonly available nearly everywhere all year long in the U.S. these days, so if they're going to fit into a microfarm, you're going to have to grow the more unusual ones.

'Bhut Jolokia' superhot pods on the plant.
Photo by Harald Zoschke.

Pros

Growing superhot chile peppers outdoors during the summer can produce valuable pods and seeds and various value-added products like powders and sauces. Although it is possible to grow chiles under artificial light or in greenhouses, the yields are usually small and these cultivation methods are not recommended. So, like tomatoes, they are a summer crop. Successful chile microfarmers focus on the superhot chiles that approach a heat level of one million Scoville Heat Units (compare the jalapeño at about 4,000 SHU), or on raising bedding plants for sale to gardeners. See the stories on

Marlin Bensinger and Cross Country Nurseries in Part 2. Chiles are about as easy to grow as tomatoes, and there are culinary varieties and ornamental ones, but the microfarmer should focus on growing either the superhots or culinary varieties that are in high demand at the time. If you live in an area that produces a lot of chile peppers, like I do, it just doesn't make any sense to grow the same varieties that the farmers with fifty acres or more are growing—they will beat you every time.

Cons

Except for the superhots, chile peppers are not a high-value crop, and that's why they are grown in such quantity on large farms. They are susceptible to a number of ravaging diseases which can destroy entire fields. The two most damaging, in my experience, are the curly top virus, transmitted from weeds by leafhoppers, and Phytophthora, a fungal disease associated with agriculture that is triggered by excessive water and causes the plants' roots to rot. Chiles are notorious for natural cross-breeding, usually by honey bees, that creates hybrids, so saving seed yourself is problematic when you are growing more than one variety. Think of un-neutered poodles and cocker spaniels frolicking around together, and then imagine the resulting cockapoo puppies and you'll get the concept.

Bottom Line

I detail in Part 4 how I experimented with growing superhots to see if they would make a good microfarm crop for my operation, and decided they would not. However, I did not attempt to create any value-added products from them, nor did I attempt to sell their seeds, which have a high value. Products may be the key for chile pepper profitability on a microfarm, but this begs the question: can I grow enough quantity to keep the products in stock? Possible products involve powders, hot sauces, salsas, and pickled peppers, but if any of those are successful you may find yourself spending most of your time processing, your microfarm may become a licensed commercial kitchen, and instead of growing, you will be sourcing the chiles from other growers. That is called the evolution of a real business, and it could make you a retired microfarmer. In three years of growing superhot chile peppers on one acre, Marlin Bensinger and I made a profit only one year, the first, and that profit was less than $20,000 and we had no value-added products.

About the Crop

As early as 1998, horticulture extension agents were pushing culinary herbs as a "viable cash crop for small-scale farmers." Two extension agents from Ohio State University conducted a survey that year of chefs in Cincinnati and found that "chefs were eager to purchase locally-grown herbs." The survey showed that the ten most popular herbs the chefs wanted were parsley, basil, chives, dill, mints, rosemary, thyme, oregano, tarragon, and French sorrel. And they wanted them to be organic and just-picked. Most chefs said they would buy one to two pounds of their favorites each week, but some of them would buy more parsley and basil—three to six pounds weekly.

Extension agents are trained to express crop values by acre, so their survey of field basils in 1998 showed a top value of $11,280 per acre or about $4.00 per pound. That would mean more than a ton of herbs that the farmer would have to constantly move down the line before it all spoiled. Of course, a microfarmer would not raise an acre of basil—most would grow herbs in containers, raised beds, or small garden plots.

Pros

Herbs are easy and inexpensive to grow, and there are so many different kinds used in cooking that the grower will not get bored with an herb crop. They are pleasant to look at, smell good, and enhance the flavor of cooked food. Although drying herbs is an effective and convenient way to preserve them, drying severely reduces the essential oils that give them their aromas and flavors, so growers should examine other preservation methods like freezing, or making value-added products like pestos, oils, vinegars, or compound butters.

A professional greenhouse like this one in Parma, Italy, can be used to grow culinary herbs year-round.
Photo by Dave DeWitt.

Cons

Herbs are susceptible to insect pests like aphids, white flies, and spider mites, particularly in a winter greenhouse, and growers will have a difficult time combating them. The best organic methods are mechanical. Flypaper strips work very well for white flies and aphids, and spider mites can be washed off the plants with strong streams of water. If you have bad infestations, you might have to wash the plants two or three times a week. Harvested herbs have to be used within a short period of time, so storing them in the refrigerator only works for a few days. Chefs will reject wilted, partially dried, or brown herbs—they must be freshly picked.

Bottom Line

The Ohio extension agents made some good points in their herb report: "Marketing of herbs is much more difficult than producing them," they wrote. "Growers with great marketing skills will have a much better chance of success." Growers should always befriend chefs, eat at their restaurants, and occasionally "gift" them with supposedly excess herbs, tomatoes, or unusual plants. And there are other herb marketing opportunities beyond restaurant chefs, such as health food stores, grocery stores, farmers' markets, charity fundraisers, and food manufacturing companies. Read my story of growing herbs for an Italian chef in Santa Fe in Part 4 for more ideas. Unless you plan to start your own bottled herb company, you might want to incorporate herbs into a microfarm growing other crops.

In the winter, chefs and retailers have much more difficulty sourcing fresh herbs, so that's one of the reasons why I recommend that serious microfarmers have a small greenhouse. Growing fresh herbs in containers in the greenhouse will make them available all year long, and thus the microfarmer becomes a much more valuable resource to chefs and retailers.

About the Crop

In late 2009, *The Wall Street Journal* reported, "Decades after most small dairies were forced out of business in New York, a new crop of boutique dairies is springing up in the state to produce fancy cheese, milk and yogurt." Note that these dairies depend upon value-added products to survive, so often these dairies are family-owned farms with a handful of cows, goats, or sheep that can produce the basic ingredient for making premium dairy products: milk, and fresh milk, right from the animal and not shipped from somewhere else. A good example is Rose Marie Belforti of Finger Lakes Dexter Creamery in King Ferry, New York. She owns and milks just seven Dexter cows, a small heritage breed, to make two kefir cheeses (similar to brie) that sell for $26 to $28 a pound. The key to her sales is educating and entertaining her customers and potential customers about her unusual, pint-sized cattle that are sometimes mistaken for goats.

An Arapawa Island dairy goat on a farm.
Photo by Jennifer Dickert.

Pros

Consumers do want organic, hand-crafted dairy products like cheese and yogurt, and are willing to pay premium prices. Again, it is value-added products that will produce the largest profits. Dairying is quite satisfying, especially for people raised on farms, as it requires a knowledge of farm animals and how to care for them. Often, small dairies are combined with chicken farming for eggs, and meat goats, sheep, and cattle. If you think back to the days before gigantic corporate mono-crop farms, a cow or two was considered essential to having a productive farm.

Cons

If you have a field with grass you can raise small numbers of goats, sheep, or cows, but it is usually necessary to supplement their feed with hay during the summer and all of the winter. And hay can be expensive, especially during times of drought.

With the U.S.D.A. so concerned about the risks of salmonella and *E. coli*, you will have to keep very accurate batch statistics, and you will probably be inspected by your state department of agriculture, which will likely require licensing. Animals require care, so there will be vet bills and the cost of medicines. You will need equipment including refrigeration, which can be a large investment. There is also quite a learning curve to running a dairy, and a lot of things can go wrong. And you will have to have a good plan for dealing with animal waste. Obviously, a small dairy is not for the average microfarmer.

Bottom Line

If you were raised on a farm, especially a dairy farm, and love animals, a microdairy may be the farm for you. Explore your state's agricultural college or extension service for dairy courses you can take or audit, or you could apprentice to someone who has a dairy. I would advise not attempting this on your own—get experienced help. Value-added products are essential to a successful microdairy, and the highest value products are unique cheeses, ice creams, and flavored yogurts. And be sure that your business plan has branding, marketing, and advertising as important and absolutely necessary expenses. A unique selling proposition beyond organic, free-range animals will be a necessity. The mini-cows mentioned above, for example, could be the stars of an advertising campaign like "Big, Bold Cheeses from Pint-Sized Cows."

About the Crop

The most economically important non-tropical fruit crops are apples, peaches, pears, apricots, plums, and cherries. The most important berry crops worldwide include strawberries, blueberries, cranberries, black currants, table and wine grapes, raspberries, and blackberries. For a microfarm, working with fruits and berries will definitely involve value-added products, since you will never be able to compete with large produce companies for fresh fruits or berries, except in you-pick operations where fruit buying becomes a family adventure. So think fruit leathers, jams, jellies, preserves, and fruit-based barbecue sauces.

Pros

Fruits are perennials and don't have to be replanted each year. They also produce high yields, which can result in a lot of value-added products. Albuquerque has a couple of companies that illustrate how a fruit and berry microfarm could work. The first one, Urban Orchards, is a fruit rescue company, and its business plan revolves around finding neglected, unharvested

fruit trees and working a deal with the owners to share the fruit and make products with it. Members of this small "co-op" not only enjoy the warm and fuzzy feeling of being part of a local, sustainable business, but also receive shares of the final product made from their own trees. The second example is Heidi's Raspberry Farm, which is profiled in Part 2, and depends on both products and the you-pick concept for their profits. If you have a couple of acres, you can grow an amazing volume of fruit in a small area.

Strawberries, blueberries, and blackberries.
Photo by Scott Bauer, USDA ARS.

Cons

It takes years to establish even a small orchard, so time will be a factor in your plan. Many fruits and berries will not set fruit if there is frost on their flowers, so an entire crop could be ruined by a late freeze. This happened in 2013, when a late frost hit the South Valley, wiping out all the peaches, apples, and plums in the orchard I walk by a couple of times a week. Only some pears survived. Fruits and berries are quite perishable, so they have to be processed quickly, with the possible exception of apples, which have the longest "shelf-life." Picking, sorting, and processing fruit is very labor-intensive and time consuming. Also, because of pests like borers that can kill fruit trees, it is extremely difficult to raise fruits organically.

Bottom Line

If you have fruit trees or berry brambles already, you can do some experimentation without much expense or risk. If you're going to have to plant small trees or berry canes and create an orchard, you'd better have a brilliant business plan or it's probably not worth the investment, time, and trouble. Heidi Eleftheriou makes a number of different kinds of raspberry jams, with a ten-ounce jar selling for $7.99 in 2014, so she has to have a big harvest every year to make a profit. As with having a microdairy, a micro-orchard is not for everyone and might turn out to be more of a labor of love than a labor for profit.

About the Crop

According to the Fresh Garlic Association, garlic is the second most-used spice in the entire world and every year Americans consume over three hundred million tons of garlic. With prices as high as $7.00 a pound for gourmet garlic, and its long storage time, garlic is a top crop to consider growing. It is one of the easiest and most profitable crops to grow on a small farm. It is an excellent crop for a diversified microfarm that grows a number of different crops. There is a saying that garlic should be planted on the shortest day of the year and harvested on the longest. But you don't have to wait until December twenty-first to plant your cloves; any time from mid-fall on is fine. This growing cycle does not interfere with raising the typical summer crops. Elephant garlic is a bulb that's related to the leek but its appearance, growth habits, and garlic flavor are more garlic-like than leek-like. Elephant garlic is less cold-hardy than common garlic plants, grows a bit bigger, and is harder to find—which makes it more valuable.

The best places to market garlic for small growers include farmers' markets, roadside stands, mail-order sales, produce brokers, supermarkets, organic food distributors, and food co-ops, and growers should consider making value-added products including pastes and powders that feature specific varieties.

Garlic bulbs.
Photo by Rüdiger Wölk.

Pros

Up to one acre of elephant garlic produces fifteen thousand pounds of salable product. Growing elephant garlic for a profit is not extremely labor-intensive, and will help dedicated gardeners make a good profit. On an organic microfarm where much of the work is done by hand, garlic is a good crop because it is space-efficient, easy to plant and harvest, and easy to handle during the cleaning and curing process. Garlic has relatively few pests and diseases due to its anti-fungal and anti-bacterial properties and many growers actually use garlic solutions as pest control on their other crops—it does, in fact, repel aphids. Garlic can be successfully

grown using furrow, sprinkler, or drip irrigation. However, because garlic has a relatively shallow root system, it is sensitive to moisture stress throughout the growing season.

The hardneck varieties of garlic plants send up a central flower shoot called a scape. The scape can be harvested and sold because it provides a tasty garlic product in the spring, when no other fresh garlic is available. Once the bulbs are harvested, cleaned, and dried, they may be moved to long-term storage locations. Garlic will usually store well for eight months or more if kept cool and dry.

Cons

Growing garlic can be surprisingly difficult at times, especially if the wrong diseases hit your crop at the wrong time. White rot fungus or nematodes can easily wipe out a garlic field. The cost of seed cloves plus the hand labor for planting and harvest makes the initial investment for garlic production high in comparison to some other vegetable crops. Weeds are a major concern for farmers wherever garlic is grown. It requires nearly perfect weed control since it emerges slowly and never forms a shade canopy with its short, vertical leaf arrangement. The long growing season required for garlic production subjects garlic to competition from successive cycles of weed growth. It also takes two weeks to cure once it's been harvested.

Bottom Line

According to University of Minnesota Extension Service, in their publication "Growing Garlic in Minnesota," garlic can be a profitable crop for vegetable growers with average yields of 8,000-10,000 pounds per acre, and prices ranging from $5.00 to $10.00 per pound at farmers' markets. Another university source notes that an acre of well-managed conventional or organic garlic that is directly marketed at prime locations by the producer (perhaps in braids and other forms) could return in excess of $5,000 per acre. I could easily incorporate garlic into my microfarm of tomatoes, superhot chile peppers, and culinary herbs. I would just build additional raised beds for garlic and probably would rotate it with tomatoes.

About the Crop

Of all the microfarm crops discussed in this book, ginseng is the most confusing and in some ways, the most suspicious. The value of this woodland root herb varies wildly according to which source you consult, and I found the supposed price per pound for growers swinging from $50 to $700. It seems sometimes like it's a get-rich-not-so-quick scheme because you must wait ten years for the crop to mature. Or five years. Or three years, depending on the source you consult, and apparently, the growing techniques you use. All of this conflicting information was getting irritating, so I decided to go directly to the state that grows the most of it — Wisconsin.

Ginseng is prized in Asia for its purported curative properties. Its genus name, Panax, is derived from the Greek *panakeia*, which means universal remedy or a panacea. It is used in teas, lotions, and soaps, and there's no surprise that most of the Wisconsin ginseng crop is exported to China, Taiwan, and Japan, where it is then redistributed to other locations in the Far East. The remainder of the crop is retailed as dried roots, sliced roots, powder, and capsules. On one website, the price of a pound of ginseng powder is $52, while whole roots were going for three times that price. On another site, the large roots were selling for $174 a pound in four-ounce gift boxes. Apparently, extremely high prices are only for

Ginseng harvest in Walsrode, Germany.
Photo by Katharina Lohrie.

very large and very old roots, something that the typical microfarmer would not have time for. But why the high prices to begin with? It's all about habitat.

Ginseng is a woodland crop that requires seventy to ninety percent natural or artificial shade. It thrives in a climate with forty to fifty inches of rain a year and an average temperature of fifty degrees Fahrenheit. It requires several weeks of very cold temperatures for adequate dormancy. In Wisconsin, most growers harvest ginseng the third year after planting from seed, and this shortened growth period is why the

prices are lower than the exaggerated quotes. The roots are dug up in the fall and vigorously washed to remove surface soil.

There are two main methods of ginseng cultivation. Field cultivated ginseng is grown in raised beds in fields under artificial shade provided by either wood lathing or polypropylene shade cloth for a period of three to four years. Patient growers can harvest considerably larger quantities using the "wild-simulated" growing method, in which you plant it in the woods, leave it alone for five or seven years, and then dig it up and retire. Supposedly.

Pros

According to WildGrown.com, "The current price [is] $400 or more per pound. It will cost about $1500 per acre to plant ginseng, and after ten years, you will harvest over $100,000 worth of ginseng per acre. It is inflation proof, which means it is not affected by US economy or subject to the Federal interest rate." That optimistic appraisal will only apply to certain ginseng growers, but still, high quality ginseng roots bring very high crop prices when compared to others. The only major work involved is in planting and harvesting. Planting is a lot of work, but you only have to do it once. Harvesting also is a lot of work but you can hire a large crew at a fairly low cost. The rest, monitoring and care, is easy and does not take much time.

Cons

Its limited habitat is so specialized that most microfarmers will have to use raised beds with shading rather than the wild-simulated methods. State regulations on growing ginseng vary, and in some areas you will need special permits or licenses, especially if you are growing for commercial harvest. Ginseng cultivation is deceptively simple but it's risky, too. The crop can be stolen by humans or eaten by rodents. It is important to remember that ginseng, and particularly ginseng under cultivation, is a plant prone to many diseases, most of them fungal. And although the length of time until harvest varies, it still takes a long time for ginseng to reach a harvestable size. One source says five to twelve years when planted from seed, and two to four years if started from transplants.

Bottom Line

Since ginseng prices vary widely, prospective growers will want to contact ginseng growers in their area to get a more accurate local picture of income potential. Dennis Lindberg of Ozark Mountain Ginseng in Missouri says that "knowing your market, or where you will sell the ginseng, is critical." Dennis sells his seedlings and transplants at several locations in feed stores and farm centers. He also sells the mature roots to a buyer who resells them to medicinal companies. He can sell his seedlings and transplanted roots for $1.00 to $2.00 each. The price of ginseng varies depending on whether it is wild-simulated or cultivated. The wild is more valuable but also harder to find. Dennis says the price he gets varies between $100 to $250 per pound of dried roots. Perhaps the point we should remember here is that high crop prices alone are just one consideration when choosing a microfarm crop. In this case, habitat needs, risk, and a ready market are even more important considerations.

SPECIALTY SALAD MIXES

About the Crop

The "microgreening of America," as one food writer termed it, has evolved from a minor amount of small greens used as a garnish by chefs in upscale restaurants to a cottage industry, where the "cottage" is a small greenhouse with a rack or shelving system designed for vertical space efficiency. Several pounds of microgreens can be grown per square foot per month, and with this organic, specialty produce selling for $25 a pound or more, microfarmers specializing in greens can make a good supplementary income. Some of these mixed greens include amaranth, arugula, beets, basil, celery, chard, cilantro, kale, various types of lettuce, mustard, parsley, radish, and spinach.

Pros

Easy to grow, microgreens can be ready to sell in ten to twenty days. They are a good greenhouse crop in the winter, and it doesn't cost a lot of money to start this operation. I will cover the type of greenhouse to build in Part 3, but a small greenhouse should be a part of every microfarming operation. For example, you can grow microgreens and culinary herbs together during the winter, and then switch to starting the seeds for your outdoor microfarm operation.

Cons

The usual pests of the winter greenhouse — namely whitefly, aphids, and spider mites — might give you trouble, and the important thing here

Microgreens at Lufa Farms, the world's first commercial rooftop greenhouse, in Montreal, Canada.
Photo courtesy of Lufa Farms.

is not to allow an infestation to get established. It is important that your microgreens be totally organic, because that will distinguish them from the less expensive salad mixes sold by supermarkets. You will need to carefully inspect the greens every day, use flypaper strips to trap flying insects, and always check under the leaves, because that's where the infestations stop. Although heating the greenhouse is important, greens don't mind cooler temperatures in the forties, so make sure the temperatures don't fall to freezing. Moving air and ventilation are very important at all times, but especially when the sun heats up the greenhouse during the day. Also, to achieve the highest possible prices, you will need to give samples to chefs and make sure your packaging is unique and attractive.

Bottom Line

Although prices can vary quite a bit depending on location and season, one of the best things about growing microgreens is that they take up a very small amount of space. Fifty pounds of microgreens can be grown in a sixty square foot growing area every two weeks, and at $25 per pound, that's a return that beats just about any other legal crop. Most growers report an average harvest of five to six ounces of microgreens per single tray (10″ x 20″) when grown on a single level, such as a tabletop. And just as important, supplying needed microgreens will impress chefs, and connections to chefs are necessary for profitable farming of microgreens — but not all year long. During the outdoor growing season, you can also fashion growing beds in partially shaded areas and raise a greater volume of microgreens, but they will not do very well during the hottest part of the summer, so plan for spring and fall growing outside. In addition to microgreens, you could add culinary herbs, tomatoes, and baby vegetables like carrots and radishes to your crop as a summer salad promotion that would work at farmers' markets with your own brand of salad dressings as value-added products.

HORTICULTURAL SPECIALTIES

About the Crop

Included in this category are houseplants, bedding plants, landscaping plants, and organic specialty flowers. In Part 2 I profile Cross Country Nurseries in New Jersey, who sell five hundred varieties of chile pepper bedding plants, plus hundreds of varieties of tomatoes and eggplants, by mail order. Most landscaping nurseries are microfarms with a transient population that will soon find a permanent home. Although the fad of edible flowers has wilted, cut flowers continue to be strong sellers at excellent prices, and the "buy green" trend has sprouted new microfarms that grow perennial, organic, and heirloom flowers that florists don't carry and that customers will buy in large, unique bouquets for $250.

Pros

Specialty nurseries can produce higher profits in smaller spaces. I have mentioned several above, but the ones getting the most attention are those for native plants, which can bring high prices. If you have a love of plants and an idea good enough to write a business plan about, then one of these categories might work. Janie Lamson of Cross Country inherited a nursery from her parents and transformed it into a highly successful specialty plant supplier. Plants of the Southwest, with locations in Santa Fe and Albuquerque, has been successful in raising and supplying native plants for years. There aren't many urban flower farms, but I profile one in Part 2.

Potted chrysanthemums growing in a nursery.
Photo by Liz West.

Cons

There are no specific cons to these crops, just the usual risks and difficulties that accompany microfarming and farming in general. It is said that people in agriculture are just waiting for something good to happen, and in my experience, no season is perfect. Something bad always happens. Late freezes like I had this spring, hail, the germination failures in our Las Cruces microfarm in 2012, and so on. Curly top virus, spider mites, hornworms—even deer! Fortunately, there are solutions to many of these problems. Serious seed overplanting for twice the bedding plants you'll need is always a good idea, for example. You can buy crop insurance that covers hail.

Bottom Line

The key to success in this field is finding a specific niche for your business. Janie Lamson has been able to find hers by specializing in live chile pepper, eggplant, and tomato plants. The 2014 price for a single chile pepper bedding plant ordered from Cross Country Nurseries is $3.75, with a minimum order of six, plus shipping. And Janie sells a pack of ten superhot chile pepper seeds for $4.00. She told me that her 2014 income for the sale of live plants was up fourteen percent over 2013. In the horticultural and nursery business, you must have a niche like hers, a specialty, and a business that draws serious home gardeners and landscape consumers to it. You must know it cold, be able to answer any question about it, and use all the available, inexpensive techniques to communicate with your customers: email newsletters, a website, a blog, social media, a national press release service, as well as traditional advertising in your market, especially local newspapers and magazines that are read by home cooks and gardeners. All of these efforts will result in building a brand that will be immediately recognized by your current and future customers.

About the Crop

As of this writing in the summer of 2014, 23 states plus the District of Columbia have enacted laws to legalize medical marijuana. If you live in one of these states, check to see the status of growing it—not mere possession. If you do not live in one of these states, stop reading this section of the book because I don't want you to commit any illegal acts—it's just not worth it. In other words, don't do what I did many years ago as documented in Part 3.

This plant is both the most controversial and the most profitable plant to grow in our catalog of microfarm plants. It's also one of the easiest plants to grow, since in many natural circumstances, it's considered to be a common weed. An ancient survivor that can easily alternate between domesticated crop and maverick weed, marijuana has been an important part of world agriculture for millennia. It is valuable as non-psychoactive hemp for use in fiber manufacturing but the federal Controlled Substances Act of

1970 classifies marijuana as a Schedule I drug. So it is banned nationally, yet legal for recreational use in Washington and Colorado. It is a highly valuable medicine, helping sufferers of chronic pain, PTSD, and numerous other ailments, and a single, mature plant can be worth a thousand dollars or more. This is a murky place to grow, so I recommend it for adventurous and security-conscious microfarmers only. For more information, see my book, *Growing Medical Marijuana* (Ten Speed Press, 2012).

A marijuana urban garden grow bed.
Photo by Wes Naman.

Pros

Marijuana is not only highly profitable, it is extremely easy to grow either indoors or outdoors, and it is very tolerant of different climactic conditions. Marijuana requires high amounts of nitrogen, which is easy to apply in water-soluble form, and the more direct sunlight given it, the faster it grows and the higher the yields. For the first time in history, a majority of U.S. citizens believes that marijuana should be legalized or at least decriminalized.

Cons

As mentioned, marijuana is listed as a Schedule I controlled substance under federal law, in the same category as addictive and much more dangerous drugs like heroin and cocaine. Transporting marijuana across state lines remains a federal felony regardless of state laws legalizing its use, possession, or production. Good seeds are not only quite expensive, five dollars or more each, but they are also difficult to find, often

available only from England, Canada, or the Netherlands, and, of course, shipping marijuana internationally is illegal as well. Security is the biggest challenge for the home grower. If your state allows six plants in bloom, your crop could be worth a thousand dollars a plant or more, depending on size, and that would be quite a temptation if you have told anyone about your crop. The sativa species of marijuana can grow more than fifteen feet tall, making concealment very difficult. Despite the fact that it is relatively easy to grow, in domestic cultivation, particularly indoors, marijuana is attacked by many common pests and is particularly susceptible to spider mites and aphids. The world of marijuana growing is still semi-underground and there is always the potential for danger and paranoia. Another drawback is registering as a medical marijuana grower in whatever state you live in because then you will be part of a database of growers that federal officials have access to. You become part of a large monitoring system, and this disturbs many people who would otherwise grow it, like refugees from the '60s. Like me. Finally, the most valuable parts of the plant are the flowering tops, inaccurately called "buds" in

Marijuana seeds.
Photo courtesy of Sunbelt Archives.

stoner vernacular, which must be cured before the tops are dried and smoked. Curing is the process that removes chlorophyll from the flowers, improving the aroma and flavor of the tops when they are smoked. Care must be taken or the entire crop could mold.

Bottom Line

Marijuana production is subject to the same market conditions as any other crop—when supplies are scarce, the price is high, and when the market is flooded, like when the crops come in during the fall, the price drops quite a bit. The Trans-High Market Quotations, found in each monthly issue of *High Times* magazine, list marijuana prices by "strain" and city across the country, and a recent issue showed a wide variation in pricing, from $150 an ounce in Oregon to $480 an ounce in Arizona, and both of these states allow medical marijuana. Having grown marijuana illegally, and witnessed it being grown and sold legally, it was an easy decision for me to make *not* to grow it. I don't have adequate security, don't want the worry involved in growing the crop, and already the price for an ounce of very high quality "Super Lemon Haze" has dropped to $200 an ounce, making it easier to buy than to grow. And as crops are smuggled in from nearby Colorado, where it is now legal to possess or grow marijuana for recreational use, the price may drop so much as to make growing unprofitable for the microfarmer. There are value-added products you can make, especially marijuana-infused foods for those who cannot or prefer not to smoke, but then you must figure out how to accomplish that according to the laws

Super Lemon Haze.
Photo courtesy of Sunbelt Archives.

of the state where you live. And not sell it by mail! Marijuana brownies are considered passé, and they have evolved into a product called Cheeba Chews™, which are like hash-oil Tootsie Rolls® that retail for up to $18 apiece and cost just a small fraction of that to produce. Other value-added products include concentrates or extractions ranging from hashish to the more modern "dabs," "shatters," and "sugars." I should point out, though, that making extracts requires specialized equipment and lessons in marijuana chemistry. The website TheGreenCross.org sells thirty Medical Cannabis Coconut Oil Capsules for $175, which is an example of a high-priced value-added product.

About the Crop

The specialty mushroom market in the United States is growing due to increased consumer demand. Oyster mushrooms are considered the easiest species to grow, but other viable mushrooms for the microfarmer include crimini, portobello, oyster, shiitake, and white button. Mushrooms prefer dark, cool, moist, and humid growing environments. In a house, a basement is often ideal, and other structures work well too, like garages, sheds, and even small warehouses. All commercial mushroom production uses a growing medium called a substrate, a sort of bedding or compost, such as sawdust or straw. The substrate or compost must be "spawned" or inoculated with mushroom mycelium that must then be allowed to develop in the compost mixture. Pennsylvania is the top-producing mushroom state in the United States, and celebrates September as "Mushroom Month." The state supplied sixty-four percent of U.S. production, with California second at thirteen percent.

Pros

You can grow mushrooms in as little as a few dozen square feet, and a lot of times that space is not well-used anyway, like basements or garages. Indoor tray growing is the most common commercial technique, followed by growing in containers that can be as simple as plastic bags filled with sterilized, wet substrate and spawn. The tray technique provides the advantages of scaling up your growing and easier harvesting. Growing indoors gives you more environmental control, and the harvests are more predictable

Agaricus bisporus being grown at Ostrom's Mushrooms, Mushroom Corner, Lacey, Washington.
Photo courtesy of the Mushroom Observer.

than in outdoor scenarios. With six crop cycles per year, a two-hundred square foot grow space will yield five to six thousand pounds of oyster mushrooms a year. The average yield for button mushrooms over a fifteen-week cycle is typically three pounds per square foot, including substrate production time. One easy way to get started is with a mushroom cultivation kit; they are readily available from online suppliers. Fresh mushrooms have never been implicated in any outbreaks of foodborne illness, says Laura Phelps, president of the Washington, D.C.-based American Mushroom Institute.

Cons

Because mushrooms require a high humidity, between sixty-five and ninety-five percent, many parts of the country are not well suited for mushroom farms, such as the desert Southwest. In most mushroom growing operations, fans, humidifiers, misters, and heating or air conditioning are often needed for larger grow rooms or grow houses, which can be expensive to set up and run. Parasitic insects, bacteria, and other fungi all pose risks for the mushroom grower, particularly indoors. The relatively short shelf life of mushrooms can be problematic, so you're going to have to sell them quickly after harvest. If possible, it's best to custom-grow mushrooms for chefs and take orders that you deliver regularly.

Bottom Line

The key to making a profit with mushrooms is to work both the retail and wholesale markets. When selling at farmers' markets, you should be able to charge near-retail prices varying from $8.00 to $16.00 a pound, depending on the quality of your harvest. National bottom wholesale average is $4.00 a pound. You can wholesale mushrooms to retailers, but you'll make more money by selling directly to the consumer at farmers' markets, via mail order, or at your home. Chefs will readily buy mushrooms, but it's best to arrange these sales in advance by giving samples to selected chefs. If you decide to wholesale your crop to specialty markets, remember that they want a guaranteed supply year-round, so be careful not to over-promise what you can deliver. Experienced growers urge beginners to start modestly, learn the process thoroughly, and develop a small, reliable customer base—say, a half-dozen regular customers—as a start before you expand your growing operation. Prices vary considerably. In Ohio, fresh shiitakes are bringing $4.00 to $6.50 a pound wholesale. In San Francisco, shiitake were bringing $6.50 to $8.00 a pound. That market also reported sales of "sponge" morels from Canada at $12.50 a pound; chanterelles from Oregon at $9.00 a pound; and angel trumpets from Idaho at $8.50 a pound. It is possible to dry or freeze extra mushrooms for future sales, but the prices will not be as good as the fresh ones. Value-added products such as mushroom pâtés, sauces, and pestos will greatly increase the value of the mushrooms you grow.

About the Crop

Start researching tilapia and you'll soon discover that like ginseng, there's a lot of hype out there and a lot of people who want you to pay them to learn how to grow these fish for food and profit. Americans ate 475 million pounds of tilapia last year, four times the amount they ate a decade ago, making this once-obscure African native the most popular farmed fish in the United States. Tilapia is a hardy, warm-water fish. Compared to other fish, it is easy to grow and manage and you can grow tilapia in tanks or ponds if you can keep the water warm enough. What is your plan after harvesting your fish? You have two options to choose from—use the crop for household food consumption or sell it to retailers or local markets. There's a giant aquaponics project in a Chicago warehouse that feeds the fish on spent grain from the brewery on site, uses the fish water to grow herbs and greens, and serves them in a locavore restaurant.

Pros

Tilapia do well in poor water quality, requiring relatively low-cost feeds. They grow quickly in ponds or tanks. These fish are popular in grocery stores and markets. To raise them, you can have something as simple as four 55-gallon barrels or a larger, affordable 275-gallon food-grade tote to create an excellent ecosystem to raise tilapia. One aquaponic setup uses fish waste to grow mint and basil.

Cons

Tilapia are a non-native species and are regulated in Florida and other states. One large issue in aquaponics is the uncontrolled reproduction of tilapia in the system, which eventually leads to overcrowding and stunted growth. Another major problem with tilapia is that they are a very invasive species. If they

Tilapia swimming in a large tank.
Photo courtesy of Sunbelt Archives.

escape into local water that doesn't fall below sixty degrees, they'll pretty much take over any freshwater body of water. Tilapia are not cold-hardy fish, and the temperature range for optimal growth is eighty-four to eighty-eight degrees Fahrenheit. Mortality is high when temperatures dip below fifty degrees Fahrenheit for several days.

Bottom Line

Known in the food business as "aquatic chicken" because it breeds easily and tastes bland, tilapia is the perfect factory fish; it happily eats pellets made largely of corn and soy and gains weight rapidly, easily converting a diet that resembles cheap chicken feed into low-cost seafood. You would have to learn how to clean and fillet them for sale, plus refrigeration and packaging, and you would have to have the proper permits and inspection for wholesaling the fish to retailers and restaurant chefs. The best analysis of profits from tilapia farms is from the University of Florida. Their studies indicated that a hypothetical six-acre tilapia culture facility required an initial investment of $65,850 and generated $40,259 in annual operating costs, yielding $29,221 in net returns during an average year. Raising tilapia is a specialized business and is not for everyone, but if you live in a warm climate, you might want to give it a try. But first, visit some tilapia farms and check them out to see if they would work in your plan.

About the Crop

"With the possible exception of the apple," writes Cary Fowler, executive director of the Global Crop Diversity Trust, "there is no food crop in North America or Europe more evocative, more capable of stirring passions and memories, than the tomato." I have to completely agree with this statement, having been a lifelong devotee of the Tomato Cult, and a tomato cultivator for more than sixty years. No wonder it was the principal crop of my backyard microfarm experiment, detailed in Part 4. Tomatoes are America's number one garden crop, and U.S. farms produced $1.3 billion worth of them on 105,700 acres in 2009.

Everyone thinks that heirloom tomatoes are the be-all and end-all of gardening, but Brendan Borrell, writing in *Scientific American*, stated that most aficionados believe that "heirlooms must have a more diverse and superior set of genes than their grocery store cousins, those run-of-the-mill hybrid varieties such as beefsteak, cherry and plum." He's right—I thought the same thing.

But apparently I was wrong. "No matter how you slice it," he added, "their seeming diversity is only skin-deep: heirlooms are actually feeble and inbred—the defective product of breeding experiments that began during the Enlightenment and exploded thanks to enthusiastic backyard gardeners from Victorian England to Depression-era West Virginia. Heirlooms are the tomato equivalent of the pug—that 'purebred' dog with the convoluted nose that snorts and hacks when it tries to catch a breath." I know, it's gardening heresy, but with the exception of the 'Black from Tula,' described below, hybrids consistently have produced larger yields than heirlooms in my microfarm.

The perfect tomato. Hand model: Mary Jane Wilan.
Photo by Dave DeWitt.

Pros

Tomatoes can produce a bumper yield like no other crop. Unexpectedly, a planting of an heirloom variety 'Black from Tula' produced a gigantic harvest one season from just six plants, and my wife and I had to scramble to preserve them all, and ended up giving away a third of the crop. I had a microfarm then and didn't even realize it. They come in colors from yellow to nearly black; their sizes vary from miniature varieties less than an inch long to a whopper I grew one year that weighed a pound and a half. Their versatility in cooking is unmatched by any other fruit or vegetable, and the gift of a perfectly shaped, bright red and ripe half-pound tomato is treasured by anyyone who is a food lover. If you know what you're doing, by harvesting all the green tomatoes in your garden after the first mild frost, you can extend the fresh tomato season well into December. By turning a lot of your ripe tomatoes into puree, you can bring them back with a sauce encore in January and February. They are truly one of the best crops to grow in your microfarm. But can you make any money with them?

Cons

Tomatoes can be a spectacular failure like no other crop. I've felt the infinite sadness of watching the plants wither and die from the curly top virus, of returning from a brief vacation to find entire plants stripped of leaves by tomato hornworms, and of growing a large tomato plant that never set fruit because of blossom drop. Tomatoes are a little unpredictable and using the same varieties, the same techniques, and the same care, I have good years and average years and poor years. The best advice to conquer this is plant three times the number of seeds you think you'll need, just in case. And unlike chile peppers, tomatoes do not grow particularly well in containers unless they are very small-fruited. Keep in mind that if you try to sell your tomatoes at the growers' market, you could be in competition with as many as ten or twenty other growers, and shoppers will invariably buy the biggest and least blemished tomatoes first, so you'll have to figure out a better way to market them.

Bottom Line

Here's a quick tomato profit calculator: Allowing the usual six square feet per plant, with an average yield of twenty-five pounds per plant and a price of $4.00 per pound for heirloom tomatoes, that's more than $16.00 per square foot of garden, which is excellent. Be sure to choose varieties that are indeterminate, which means they will bloom and set fruit continually during the season. Determinate tomatoes all flower and fruit at the same time, which is often inconvenient. Despite the magic of the term "heirloom" tomatoes, those varieties grow well, but they are not as prolific as hybrid tomatoes. I think value-added tomato products are the answer to the tomato competition problem. Have a favorite bartender? Why not produce some fresh Bloody Mary mix for his or her bar? You can make and jar varietal pasta sauces, or sun-dry or dehydrate thin slices of tomatoes, then grind them into tomato powder, which retails at $4.40 for a 3.5-ounce jar. The drawback to this product is the fact that tomatoes are ninety percent water. More about these value-added options in Part 4.

PART 2

14 FEATURED MICROFARMERS
and 1 BIG BUYER

I have chosen to profile these microfarms because of their diversity in both crops grown and the techniques used to grow them. From mushrooms to oysters, raspberries to chile peppers, people grow the crops they love the most. Microfarms are a return to an early American tradition of self-reliance and entrepreneurship in the face of monocultural factory farms operating today.

For Chispas Farms, It All Began with Garlic

Amanda and Eli Burgione have been full-time microfarmers since 2003, generating all of the family income from their farm. They grow heirloom garlic, shallots, tomatoes, sweet peppers, herbs, sweet potatoes, and winter squash on about two and a half acres in the South Valley of Albuquerque.

Eli dropped out of the University of Chicago after two years because he felt he was not learning about real life. So he spent a couple of years hitchhiking around the U.S. and working on all types of farms to learn growing, well, from the ground up. This was real, and he loved it. When the opportunity arose for him to return to his hometown of Albuquerque and be

Eli Burg of Chispas Farms
Photo courtesy of Chispas Farms.

the grower and manager of an organic microfarm, he and his wife, Amanda, jumped at the chance.

They began in the first years by growing out varieties of every high-value crop they could until they found the ones that did the best in their soil and microclimate, and the ones that would generate the most income for the least amount of time, effort, and space. They settled on heirloom organic garlic varieties because they could sell each head retail for either seventy-five cents or a dollar, and in 2011 they grew 45,000 heads on a half-acre. The staggered harvest runs from May through July. They sell the garlic at farmers' markets, vegetable fairs, and to restaurants. The garlic seeds are provided to Seed Savers Exchange.

The other crops are high-value as well, like culinary herbs (basil, sage, thyme, oregano), specialty tomatoes, and multi-colored sweet peppers. Their principal winter crop is winter squash, and the other beds are planted with cover crops like oats and winter wheat that are not harvested but rather plowed under in the spring to enrich the soil. They have a greenhouse and small tractor and believe in integrating the crops and rotating them throughout the farm every year. They use staggered planting to achieve staggered harvests of all crops so everything doesn't get ripe at the same time. They have one assistant gardener and one intern, but during harvest season they throw Harvest Parties, where neighbors and friends assist in picking and get a percentage of what they pick. Eli reports that many beer cans turn up during spring plowing.

Eli and Amanda believe in coexisting peacefully with their neighbors of every species. For example, the house on the property was plagued by mice, but instead of trapping them, Eli built them a new home about fifty yards away. He made a large pile of tree branches and brush and now provides five pounds of dried corn each year. The mice moved to paradise, except for dealing with the farm cats. Eli says beginning microfarmers should start small and build up, learning as they go what crops to grow and how to sell them. They should continue experimentation even after they have developed a profitable microfarm. Growers should always have a special crop that appeals to them and be the best at growing it. They should not think negatively about drudge work like weeding — scheme while you weed, think of more ways the farm can generate money, suggests Eli. "A big part of sustainability," he says, ever the entrepreneur, "is not killing yourself by working too hard. Constantly be thinking of ways to work less to make more income off your microfarm." Eli's garlic yield is twice that of California garlic farms.

A Chilli Farm in Cardiff, Wales

Chilli pepper (U.K. spelling) microfarmer Chris Fowler has his Dragon Chilli Farm in a polytunnel because, as he puts it, the weather in Cardiff, South Wales, is mostly miserable, with too much rain and not enough sunshine. But still, he manages to grow chillis and other crops successfully in 1,404 square feet, earning about one-third of the family income from his farm. He uses city water to irrigate his chillis, potatoes, onions, shallots, garlic, lettuce, cabbage, celery, cauliflower, beans, peas, carrots, kale, leeks, strawberries, parsnip, spring onions, blueberries, squash, and courgettes (zucchini). Chris' diverse microfarm is a good example of an arrangement to use someone else's under-used space.

His interest in growing chilli peppers began around 2004, he told me. He had never eaten a

Chris Fowler of Dragon Chilli Farm, in his polytunnel.
Photo courtesy of Chris Fowler.

fresh jalapeño pepper (they're not available in the U.K.'s supermarkets), but he found some seeds on the internet and grew them with great success. He commented that like many growers and fans of eating lots of spicy food, you start with one variety and soon get the urge to try more.

By 2007 Chris had a house full of a few dozen varieties and had the idea to see if he could turn his hobby into a small business. For this he needed to buy a polytunnel to grow them in the U.K. climate and he was soon fortunate enough to find somewhere to put it. A personal solar panel company named G24i (also in Cardiff) was looking for someone to take over looking after their vegetable garden in their factory grounds, in exchange for space to grow vegetables. After his meeting with them, they were pleased about having him take over and adding a polytunnel measuring seventy-eight by eighteen feet within their fenced factory grounds. By early summer 2009 it was up and his first season as a microfarmer began.

His goal was to grow enough fresh produce to sell to local shops, as well as doing a regular weekly stall at Cardiff's farmers' markets, Chris told me. He'd also save a certain percentage of produce that would be kept aside and frozen to make hot sauce. As a part-time library worker, he had enough time on his own to put into the business to make it work and supplement his income with the proceeds of selling both fresh chillies/sweet peppers and homemade hot sauce. Doing all the work on his own also helped to keep him fit, which was an added bonus! Note that Chris planned from the beginning to have value-added products.

Chris integrates his farm into the factory canteen. In the polytunnel the bulk of what's growing consists of many different types of chilli, along with sweet peppers and a small area to grow tomatoes, cucumbers, and aubergines (eggplants). Some of these he would share with the factory and they would often be in their canteen within minutes of being picked. During the summer and until late autumn he filled up boxes of fresh organic vegetables which he left in the factory canteen to be used that week. The factory's green credentials went up in 2011, as it is now powered by a full-size wind turbine, making it the only factory in the world making renewable products powered by wind.

The plan is to continue expanding the microfarm. As of 2012 the size of the vegetable patch was growing and by 2013 he hoped to expand it to an area of sixty feet by eighty feet with a combination of raised beds and ground level plots. His season for selling at the local farmers' markets (depending on how good or bad a summer they had in the U.K.), is usually from mid to late August up until late November. With the produce frozen for hot sauce, producing and selling this takes him right through to the start of the season the following year. His main areas of selling hot sauce are at the markets and through social networking websites like Facebook, where he posts photos of the latest small batches he's made, as this seems to be the quickest way for people to see them. As a result, his sauces have been sent by mail order all over the U.K., America, Canada, and mainland Europe.

New microfarmers can learn some lessons from Chris: You don't need to invest a lot of money to get started, you don't need to give up your day job, and you can expand your operation gradually.

The Mysterious Medical Marijuana Microfarmer

A word of warning: if marijuana is not legal for cultivation in your state, skip this chapter and don't grow it. In this case, no laws were broken because growing marijuana is legal for personal use in the state it was grown.

Leo Lascaux, which of course is not his real name, is semi-famous these days. I should know, since I made him that way. Leo is the star of my book, *Growing Medical Marijuana* (Ten Speed Press, 2013), and in that book I chronicled his first year of growing the herb despite the fact that he had never grown any plant before in his life, including houseplants. Marijuana is his only crop, and he has no value-added products whatsoever, even edible marijuana treats. He has made tinctures of cannabis, and experiments with producing *kief*, a concentrated form like hashish but far easier to make, and is not actively selling either one of these. He grows the state-allocated number of plants in the backyard of his city residence, which has a fairly secure wall around it, gates that lock, and a lot of other foliage that helps to conceal his crop. So far, he has never been ripped off—or, for that matter, ever been visited by any representative of the medical marijuana program that is a part of the state health department.

He doesn't need all of the marijuana he can grow and possess legally for his ailing back, so some of it he sells to friends who have other medical conditions. He earns about five percent of total family income selling it, and this practice is technically illegal in the state he lives in. But in reality these days, no one cares. With Washington and Colorado having legalized the possession of marijuana for recreational use, and another

Leo Lascaux in disguise.
Photo by Wes Naman.

seventeen states and the District of Columbia legalizing the possession and usage of medical marijuana, this means that as of this writing, 23 states plus the District of Columbia have legalized it to some degree. Use whatever cliché you wish—the cat's out of the bag, or the writing's on the wall—but the legalization of marijuana in the United States is inevitable.

Leo has no one helping him with his microfarm except for a trusted house sitter on the rare occasions he leaves town during the growing season. He does all the work himself and enjoys it, and told me that if he had more secure land, he could and would easily expand his operation. But he doesn't, and he's already using the most hidden sections of his backyard. He has grown both outdoors and indoors under lights, but he much prefers growing outdoors.

"There is a lot more light, so the plants grow faster and larger," he told me. "There are fewer insect pests outdoors, and the microfarm saves the money that would have to be spent on electricity." He still uses some indoor lights to germinate and grow seedlings, but mostly he follows the summer to fall cycle of the marijuana season, and during the winter he occasionally grows the small, auto-flowering varieties from feminized seed. Translated from growerese, that means marijuana varieties that have been developed from *Cannabis ruderalis* hybrids with flowering determined not by the shorter days of fall, but by the age of the plant. These varieties rarely exceed two feet in height and are the result of seeds that have been treated to assure that they will be females.

Leo's advice to budding marijuana microfarmers is "first, read good grow guides and then study up." He also advises that cloning of plants, rather than growing exclusively from expensive seed, works well and is easy to do. The harvest itself and the post-harvest trimming and curing of the product is "tedious, but necessary." And the number one priority of anyone thinking of growing this crop is, of course, good security. "With a large plant outdoors worth up to a thousand dollars," he told me, "you have to guard it as well as you can." But with guile, not weapons.

Lorenzo's Organic ABC Microfarm

Lorenzo Candelaria's microfarm of nearly four acres adjoins the Rio Grande in Albuquerque's South Valley, where he's the fifth-generation farmer. The ABCs are asparagus, blackberries, and chiles, his main specialty crops. He also grows culinary pumpkins of the 'Speckled Hound' variety, lettuces and chard, tomatoes, and blue corn. The farm is totally organic, and Lorenzo has taken the steps necessary to be certified as organic by U.S.D.A., a process he describes as "too expensive" but sometimes necessary as a marketing tool when the catch phrase "grown with organic techniques" is insufficient to sell his produce to high-end restaurants.

The farm generates one hundred percent of family income, and Lorenzo told me that eighty percent of what they eat comes from the farm: all they have to buy at the supermarket is coffee, sugar, flour, and presumably beer. His brother Ray raises pigs and he can trade produce for other meat. He sells his produce to restaurant owners, and his main customer is the owner of the two Farina restaurants—they specialize in gourmet pizzas, and buy a lot of tomatoes. Another source of steady income is his Saturday market at the farm. He has so many regular customers that he doesn't need to sell at the downtown Growers Market—their prices are way too high, he says. "Four bucks for a tomato? Gimme a break."

On a gorgeous October morning, I toured the farm with Lorenzo and his brother's boxer pup, Lucky, as a Cooper's hawk glided by us, and he told me some of the things he's learned while growing such varied crops. His blackberries have not produced a crop yet, but he's hopeful for next year.

"I didn't give them enough nitrogen," he told me. "I'll fix that next spring." He gave me a ripe pumpkin, and later when Mary Jane baked it with some butter and brown sugar, it tasted like butternut squash—quite delicious.

Lorenzo understands the necessity of having value-added products. He sells roasted green chile that people can peel and freeze, and makes ristras (strings of dried chiles) out of the red, mature pods. He roasts his blue corn, then mills it into *atole* (corn meal) that can be used to make tortillas or tamales. When he finally gets a blackberry crop, he will make jams and jellies with it. He already has experience with jarring jams—he collects the wild fruits of prickly pear cactus, called *tunas*, and one year made sixty half-pint jars of prickly pear jam. He sells all of these at his farm market.

He and his wife, Dora, run the farm and the market with two part-time workers, and he's going to expand by putting up a hoop house in Pajarito for more intensive winter gardening with microgreens. A hoop house is a simple, unheated greenhouse made with large metal hoops covered with polyethylene sheeting. (See Part 4 for details on building and using hoop houses for microfarms.) He may use some of the property outside the hoop house to expand the superhot chile part of his garden. He had never grown superhots before and liked the experience of growing something new.

After Marlin Bensinger and I had planted an acre of superhot chiles in Las Cruces, and the sixty-odd plants in pots and the raised bed in my backyard (see Part 4), we had some superhot seedlings still left. They were late arriving, and Lorenzo didn't even put them into the ground until the first of July, which I thought was way too late to have any kind of a crop. But Lorenzo is a good farmer, and the superhot chile plants, about five hundred of them, grew amazingly fast. To avoid the first freeze, Lorenzo had harvested pods the day before to avoid a coming frost, and he got about 150 pounds of pods from the plants, which he's going to freeze until he can sell all of them.

Lorenzo Candelaria shows off the size of his superhot chile pepper plants at his microfarm.
Photo by Dave DeWitt.

In the winter, Lorenzo operates two hoop houses about twenty by fifty feet where he grows lettuce, chard, spinach, and carrots. They are unheated but by using heavy cloth row covers each night and removing them in the morning the plants thrive, and the restaurant owners who buy from him are delighted to have locally grown produce all winter long.

Lorenzo told me the best thing he's learned from having the microfarm is water conservation. Because of the three-year drought, water has been scarce in New Mexico, so he flood-irrigated once at the beginning of the season, then switched to drip irrigation. By using flat beds with drip rather than rows and furrows, he can increase his yield by planting more densely, and do it with less water.

And his advice for future microfarmers? "It's harder work than you think," he warned, "and more complicated." Not only do you have to do the watering and weeding, but also the marketing and bookkeeping. "But the independence of working for yourself makes it all worthwhile."

The Killer Bee Guy Forages for Honey

In Part 1, I mentioned how Urban Orchards of Albuquerque works deals with fruit tree

owners to harvest their fruit and turn it into value-added products and then shares the revenue from the enterprise with the owners. The Killer Bee Guy, Reed Booth, of Bisbee, Arizona, has a similar operation involving Africanized bees and their honey, but with one big difference: he gets paid for the harvesting and keeps all the revenues from the honey-based value-added products.

Reed is a professional killer bee removal expert. His business card might as well read, "Have Bee Hood, Will Travel," because he does travel all over the country to permanently remove killer bee colonies from the properties of some very anxious and frightened homeowners. During the process, he keeps the honeycombs and brings them back to Bisbee, where the honey is extracted, purified, and packaged in jars and squeeze bottles. That is the basic product, Killer Bee Honey. He harvests about a ton of it a year from every imaginable place that killer bees choose to establish their colonies.

Next are the specialty honey products: Killer Bee Honey Butters in thirteen flavors from Awesome Almond to Luscious Lemon; Killer Bee Honey Mustards in four flavors; Killer Bee

Reed Booth, the Killer Bee Guy at work.
Photo courtesy of Reed Booth.

Whole Seed Honey Mustards in five flavors; and Killer Bee Pollen. Next up for Reed will be Killer Bee Mead as soon as he receives his Arizona license as a Farm Home Winery. These products are sold on his website (killerbeeguy.com) and in his small retail shop, Killer Bee Honey, on Main Street in Old Bisbee. The removal service and products provide one hundred percent of his family income.

For regular and seasonal help, Reed depends solely on people who want to work for him, so his entire operation is like an extended family. His chief bottler has been with him for five years, and she's so loyal that she had the superhero bee in his logo tattooed on her arm. Reed is so satisfied with his business that the only expansion he envisions is a larger retail store—eventually.

Reed's main advice to the people who want to become microfarmers is what he calls "the five-minute friendship." This means handling the customers by entertaining them. In five minutes, he smiles a lot, is very nice to everyone, educates them, makes them laugh, and takes the money that they're more than happy to give him in return for his products.

"Don't be shy," he suggests. No one comes into his shop or looks at some of the products on display on the sidewalk without Reed assaulting them with humor, and he turns the entire killer bee experience into something both fascinating and fun by appealing to their imagination.

That said, he warns people away from his line of work because it's simply too dangerous. He told me the harrowing story of a videographer who somehow, despite the protective gear, got stung on his lymph nodes and the resulting anaphylactic shock that came on so quickly that Reed had to drive him to the hospital because the ambulance would take too long to get there.

The doctor told Reed that if it had taken him two minutes longer to make the drive, the videographer would not have survived. "Don't try this at home," he warns.

Speaking of videographers, when I spoke to Reed, he was in the middle of several video shoots once again. This time, a production company was shooting a pilot for an Animal Planet series he will star in called "Killer Bee Killed." Considering Reed's sense of humor, this could be a very funny show.

Recently, Reed coined a new slogan for Old Bisbee: "We're all here because we're not all there."

Besides his sense of humor, what I like about Reed is that he's willing to take risks to achieve his goals, and not all of those risks are financial ones!

Life is Sweet at the Raines Honey Farm

Phillip Raines doesn't take the risks that Reed takes. His bees are not Africanized, and their hives are located on organic family farms across northwest Illinois and southwest Wisconsin. "With bees, it's location, location, location," he says, and that's why he moves the bees south to Mississippi in the winter. "It makes the bees build up faster in the spring when I move them back to Illinois and Wisconsin."

The honey he produces, combined with eggs from his chickens and the garden vegetables he grows, accounts for about twenty percent of the family food. The honey supplies one hundred percent of the family income—mostly because bees and their hives can produce not only honey, but beeswax. Phillip and his wife have an extensive line of honey-related products, including: honey in one-, two-, three- and five-

Beekeeper Phillip Raines with some of his charges.
Photo courtesy of Raines Honey Farm.

pound jars, cut comb honey, lavender-infused honey, peppermint-infused honey, and spun honey in small batches. The texture of spun honey has a thicker consistency than liquid honey and is more spreadable. Additional products include cinnamon-spun honey, honey candy, honey straws, gift boxes of honey products, eighteen different types of handmade beeswax candles, two kinds of lip balm, two kinds of skin lotion, eight specialty soaps for humans (like Chocolate-Coffee Honeybee-Scrubbed Soap), and a dog wash soap.

His advertising consists of public sampling and sales, word-of-mouth, his website, and social media, particularly Facebook. He wholesales his products to eighteen retail markets and eight restaurants, plus he retails his products in farmers' markets in the area and the Rockford City Market. "It's a lot of work," he admits, sometimes sixteen-hour days, but it's all been worth it for independence.

Phillip says that his beekeeping operation taught him how to run a company. "I had to learn everything from the health department to local laws," he said. And as far as advice to would-be beekeepers, he said, "Do not start a beekeeping microfarm unless you have three years of savings to fall back on. You will not make a living until you reach $100,000 in sales because expenses are so high in this business."

Cindy Lees working on oyster cages.
Photo by Albert Lees, courtesy of Lees Wharf Oysters.

Life on the Half Shell on Lees Wharf

The great American cynic, Ambrose Bierce, provided a telling definition of "oyster" in *The Devil's Dictionary* (1911): "A slimy, gobby shellfish which civilization gives men the hardihood to eat without removing its entrails." Indeed, when I was growing up in Virginia, oysters were nothing special. During the off-times when I was teaching freshman and sophomore composition and literature at Virginia Commonwealth University in Richmond, my friend Dave Linehan and I would drive over to the Rappahannock River where it enters the Chesapeake Bay and buy a bushel of freshly harvested oysters right off

the boat. That was in the early 1970s and the price per bushel was $8.00. Today, with oysters retailing for a dollar each, that same bushel would cost about $250.

There aren't any pearls in the oysters raised and sold by Cindy and Al Lees at Lees Wharf Oysters in Westport Point, Massachusetts, but there's plenty of value in them. Their oyster farm is located on the working waterfront of the historic town, where, as Cindy points out, "they are nurtured amongst our friends and neighbors in our own backyard." They have a one-acre oyster farm that is a grant site—the state of Massachusetts gave them a grant to start the farm and they first seeded it with 145,000 one-inch oysters in 2011, which was the same year they got married.

Their oysters are grown from these seed oysters in OysterGro cages, which help equalize feeding in each batch for consistent size, and in off-bottom cages. These two methods allow them to experiment with different grow-out systems. The cages are planted in waters just one mile from their wharf and they require lots of attention—flipping and cleaning cages, separating oysters that have grown too attached, building and maintaining trawl lines and other equipment. Cindy says, "the work is exhausting, multi-faceted, creative, and so much fun!" Fortunately, the far-sighted Lees couple used some of their grant money to give a grant to Roger Williams University, which pays the hourly wages of four part-time students who help them with the oysters.

Some of their oysters are sold when they're a little bigger to other oyster farmers, and when the other oysters reach market size, they are sold to a seafood broker who in turn sells them to retailers and restaurants. This means that Cindy, who has primary responsibility for the farm because Al has another business, does not have to make sales calls and peddle them out of her vehicle.

Cindy told me that on average her oyster operation generates a gross income of about $35,000 a year, but her season only runs from May to September. "If you work your beds year-round, you can earn a sustainable income," she said. "Profits depend on the size of your operation." And it's difficult to expand without more help—Cindy works seven days a week.

There are negatives and positives to oyster farming. Aside from work that can be cold, wet, and dirty, an oyster farm is expensive to launch—the equipment alone can require an investment of $100,000 or more—there's a constant learning curve. Cindy said it takes a "tenacious person" to deal with the permitting process alone. But on the positive side, "it feels good to grow products for human consumption in a way that helps the environment around our seaside wharf."

Scott Adams of Exotic Edibles of Edgewood.
Photo courtesy of *Albuquerque Local Food*.

Fungal Pâtés and Pesto

Scott Adams went from being a fire-eater in a carnival sideshow to a far less demanding career as an oyster mushroom farmer. He and Gael Fishnel grow oyster mushrooms because they're a good cash crop, they're easy to cultivate, and there's very little competition. They earn two-thirds of their family income from mushrooms grown in one of the smallest microfarms featured in this book, a mere seven hundred square feet. They have two small buildings for growing, and one quite a bit larger, and all three of the 'shroom grow rooms are enclosed and climate-controlled to ensure they have the proper temperature and humidity.

Their mushroom business is called Exotic Edibles of Edgewood, a small community just east of Albuquerque. They sell fresh mushrooms to certain high-end restaurants and to the general public by working growers' markets and through retail markets such as Whole Foods and La Montañita Co-op. Along with the fresh fungus, they now have four value-added products: two pestos, with one spiced up and flavored with chipotle chiles, plus a mushroom pesto and a mushroom hummus. The only advertising they do is personal appearances with tastings.

All the work on the mushroom microfarm is done by Scott, Gael, and one part-timer. "Mushroom growing is particularly not labor-intensive," Scott says. He and Gael devote one full day per week to the mushrooms and an additional one and a half hours every other day. But they do have one problem to solve: restaurateurs are always waiting for their fresh mushrooms and Scott wants to supply all of them on a regular, weekly basis. So they're going to build a 265-square foot grow room, which will significantly increase their production.

Scott's primary advice to would-be mushroom cultivators is "find a mentor." He was fortunate enough to have a friend who taught him most of what he knows, which reduced his learning curve considerably, maybe too much, because he and Gael had no business plan when they started. "We did it backwards," he admitted. In addition to a mentor and a business plan, he advised having adequate financing in place to launch a mushroom farm, and take business classes if you have no past entrepreneurial experience. He credits the free classes given by S.C.O.R.E., the Service Corps of Retired Executives, with teaching them the basics of starting a small business.

And those stories about keeping those mushrooms in the dark and feeding them manure? Not true, says Scott. They grow all their oyster mushrooms on sterilized straw, and Scott notes that in nature, oysters grow on fallen logs in forest shade.

Ginseng, Daffodils, and Pink Blueberries

In one of the most diversified microfarms I researched, Shady Oaks Farm in Poca, West Virginia (where the high school football team is called The Dots), plants grow both in full sun and deep shade on Chris and Leslie Burdette's three acres. The ginseng is the shady plant, and the blueberries are sunny. The other crops include native plants like goldenseal, bloodroot, cohosh, Jack-in-the pulpit, and maidenhair ferns. Chris's fruits are pink blueberries and red raspberries and his main vegetables are arugula, chard, and spinach. He and Leslie have even planted thirty thousand heirloom daffodils whose bulbs he will dig up, separate, and sell—leaving one section in the ground for the following year.

Why all the different crops? "Diversify," Chris says. "Don't expect to make a lot of money on one thing. Research what sells." Which makes a lot of sense in my opinion, mostly because farming is imprecise at best—you never know what's going to happen, so it's best to hedge your bets. This is precisely the reason they planted 'Pink Lemonade' blueberries, a variety developed by the U.S.D.A. They are striking, different, delicious, and will charm his self-picking customers, as well as the farmers' market clientele who buy from them.

In 1997, the Burdette team started their farm "as a way to eventually retire from our real jobs and stay home and make a living from here." That hasn't completely happened yet, and they work as residential window cleaners to pay about half of the bills. And it's just the two of them working the farm—they have no hired help. But they do have

value-added products, jams and jellies from the blueberries and raspberries, that they sell to farm visitors and at the farmers' markets.

Chris and Leslie grow their main product, wild-simulated ginseng roots, under a natural shade canopy in rich woods dirt. Nothing is added—no other soil, soil amendments, or fertilizer. Wild-simulated means that if it's grown properly, it will look wild, which is more valuable than garden ginseng. In addition to dried roots, they sell one-, two-, and three-year wild-simulated ginseng rootlets, as well as the seeds. When the ginseng market is good, their wild-simulated dried roots get the same price as the wild-harvested roots. The herb grows wild in all fifty-five counties in West Virginia, and the state Department of Commerce reported in 2013 that the average price for wild, dried, ginseng root was $508 per pound. But it occasionally has reached the $700 level.

The Burdettes believe that diversification and expansion will eventually free them from cleaning windows. "Research things right," advises Chris. "If you are better prepared for your growing projects, you can do it right and still take care of your land." He wants to build two more greenhouses, eventually reach ten thousand blueberry plants, and have his farm become a Certified Organic operation as soon as possible.

Chris Burdette of Shady Oaks Farm
Photo courtesy of Shady Oaks Farm.

Jennifer Hines and Pete Shrop of Rockhill Creamery.
Photo by Jeff Hunter.

Rockhill Creamery and Farmstead Cheese

Pete Shrop and Jennifer Hines based their entire business plan for Rockhill Creamery on six cows—no more and no less. "That's it!" said Jennifer. Obviously expansion is not a goal for these two former journalists who live and make cheese in Richmond, Utah. Their historic farm is merely four acres, and they lease two additional acres so each cow has its own acre. And these six cows provide the two with one hundred percent of their family income. How do they do it?

"First and foremost is the highest quality milk that our 'girls' provide," explained Jennifer. "By using raw milk (not pasteurized), we get more depth of flavor from our cultures. And then there are the months of loving care we give to each wheel of cheese as it resides in our aging cave." They offer their cheeses at three different ages; when young, their cheeses are softer and creamier with a mild flavor. They get harder and drier with a deeper, more complex flavor when older.

They have eight unique signature cheeses. Dark/Snow Canyon Edam, named for their two favorite canyons, is a semi-hard Edam that's aged between two and four months, while the Wasatch Mountain Gruyere is a light but rich-flavored, complex cheese. Belvedere Tomme is a semi-soft cheese with a rustic rind that's "stinky" in the classic French style, and their Farmhouse Gouda is offered as three different ages with the oldest called "Reserve." A variation on that is Zwitser, which is a quite strong cheese. The Peppercorn is seasoned with black pepper, the Boo Boo Baby Swiss began as a mistake (hence the name) but now is a permanent selection of the creamery. The Desert Red Feta is, of course, made with cow's milk, rather than the traditional goat's milk, and is rubbed in red salt mined in southern Utah before the blocks go into the aging brine.

Pete and Jennifer sell about eighty percent of their cheese wholesale to chefs at high-end restaurants, and some to specialty cheese shops. The remaining cheese is retailed on their website and directly to customers who visit the Rockhill

Creamery during the warm months of the year. They do no advertising, so it's just word-of-mouth working its usual magic when you have such high quality products. They do all the milking and cheese-making themselves, except when they find what they term "live-on-the-farm apprentices," an experiment that Jennifer now calls their "key to success." At the end of their term, each apprentice is paid a stipend.

Their advice for incipient dairy microfarmers? Take business classes. Research the small dairy industry. Prepare for a lot of hard work. And build a good reputation. It's a plan that has obviously worked for them at Rockhill Creamery.

The Best Organic Farmer in New Mexico

That would be Heidi Eleftheriou, the raspberry queen of New Mexico—at least in 2013, when she was awarded the title of Best Organic Farmer by the New Mexico Organic Farming Conference. And to think that when she started Heidi's Raspberry Farm, all the "experts" told her that raspberries would not grow well in New Mexico because of the dry climate. Well, they grow very well with irrigation and her supervision on five acres in Los Lunas and four acres in Corrales (not all of the land is planted with raspberries). Heidi told me that she wanted

Heidi Eleftheriou of Heidi's Raspberry Farm.
Photo by Stephanie Cameron, courtesy of *Edible Santa Fe.*

to make raspberry jam "the right way," which meant growing her own berries. Organically.

Since her husband is in the retail jewelry business, Heidi says that the farms don't provide a large percentage of their family income, but she's still trying, and income from the jams she makes from the berries is increasing. To accomplish this, she and her seasonal part-timers work farmers' markets all over the central part of the state. They wholesale the jams to grocery stores, co-ops, gift shops, bakeries, and restaurants. She works trade shows and—full disclosure here—is one of our longtime exhibitors at the National Fiery Foods & Barbecue Show. Because of her efforts over the years, she now enjoys wide distribution of her jams throughout the Rocky Mountain region.

Heidi offers you-pick baskets of fresh raspberries during the harvest season, but jams are the heart and soul of her business. She describes the jam-making process she uses at the Mixing Bowl, the community kitchen in the South Valley Economic Development Center in Albuquerque: "The jam is made in small batches, by hand, with loving care. I slowly cook the raspberries to a brief and delicate boiling phase. This method ensures that the precious vitamins and beautiful color of the natural fruit are preserved for your exquisite raspberry experience. I developed this delicious low-sugar recipe in my kitchen at home." This process results in four signature, value-added products, all called "Heidi's": Raspberry Jam, Raspberry Ginger Jam, Raspberry Red Chile Jam, and Raspberry Red Chile Ginger Jam.

"Remember, all farmers have good years and bad years," she told me. "We're all at the mercy of the weather." But with storable, value-added jams, she can survive a poor harvest because she says that "people who appreciate good food will support you if you're doing something great." She says now there's a real connection between the public and the microfarmers that did not exist when she started her business, but that doesn't matter "if you try to farm on autopilot." That's because the drought, or the bugs, or something else will "get you." You've got to be on top of the farm at all times, she says.

And her advice to people eager to microfarm berries? "Don't do it," she said jokingly. "It's too hard." But if you insist, her advice echoes that of many microfarmers. "Research value-added products and see where the markets are for yours, including websites, retailers, and shows." She warns that land is expensive to buy and to be careful with the exact arrangements if you lease land to farm. And be ready to give up your personal time because you'll have little or no time for yourself. So why do it? Why work so damned hard?

"Growing organic raspberries is an iffy business, but very satisfying," she admitted. Spoken like a true farmer.

The Six Crops of Cross Country

Janie Lamson and Fernando Villegas have one of the most unusual nurseries in the world. At Cross Country Nurseries in Rosemont, New Jersey, they raise only food plants for home gardeners and microfarmers: chile peppers, tomatoes, eggplants, basil, tomatillos, and cilantro. It sounds rather basic until you look a little deeper and realize that they sell five hundred different varieties of chile peppers, one hundred eighty varieties of tomatoes, sixty varieties of eggplants, one hundred and five varieties of basil, twenty varieties of tomatillos, and eight varieties of cilantro. The first three plants are available through their website, ChilePlants.com, and the other three are available only to walk-in traffic to their nursery.

They do this on approximately five acres of growing land that holds twelve heated hoop houses where the seeds are sprouted and the young plants are raised. Their nursery operation supplies nearly one hundred percent of family income, and they eat only a small percentage of what they grow, mostly sweet peppers and tomatoes because Janie can't take very much chile heat in her food. It's another story for Fernando, who was born in Mexico.

They opened Cross Country as a typical small nursery in 1985 and started experimenting with chile peppers in 1993. In 1997, they sold their first live plants via mail order, and by 2001 they sold only chile peppers to their online and local customers. They gradually expanded their operation to include five more plants, and now Janie says, "That's it. We're done. We've got this business figured out where we want it, and we just don't want to work any harder. No more expansion!"

And besides, they can't do it all by themselves. This seasonal business requires a lot of part-time help, an average of about eight to ten workers during a typical season that runs from January through harvest time. There is an amazing amount of things to do to manage the growing of 873 different plant varieties, and then having to ship most of them. "How did you do it?" I asked Janie.

"Slow and steady wins the race," she said. "If you get really big, really fast, and then make a mistake, you can easily lose it all—and quickly." The best thing to do, she advised, is to first decide what you really want to do and then formulate a plan to do it, tweaking it as you go along. "Don't diversify too fast and always have a plan B."

Her advice to new microfarmers is to pay your dues to create a good reputation with your customers. "This means being there dependably year after year, offering excellent customer support." For the first five years, she says, you should have an alternate funding source— savings, a real job, or possibly an investor. And

Janie Lamson of Cross Country Nurseries in Rosemont, NJ.
Photo by Rick Epstein, courtesy of www.nj.com.

Elizabeth and Roger Inman of Purple Adobe Lavendar Farm.
Photo courtesy of www.lanl.gov.

one of her best suggestions is that if you depend upon machines and technology, always have back-up equipment. She has two heaters in each greenhouse, just in case one fails. She has two computers, two printers, and three monitors. She also has an extra printer to print variety names on plastic tags and labels—which costs $5,000. "But it would take me weeks to order one and get it here if it breaks down, and that would effectively shut down my business during the shipping season. Better to be prepared and have a back-up printer." That makes sense to me.

In addition to live plants, Janie and Fernando sell organic gardening supplies, and they have some very unusual value-added products—the ripe chile pods themselves. In addition to selling live plants to gardeners all over the country, they grow out many of those plants in their own fields and offer chile pods, tomatoes, and eggplants at harvest time. It's an extra boost at the end of their season.

A Lavender Farm in Georgia O'Keeffe Country

The numbers are in on the Purple Adobe Lavender Farm in Abiquiú, New Mexico. Elizabeth and Roger Inman have 4,500 plants of fifteen different varieties of lavender on 2.5 acres of their twelve acres of land, and twenty-four different value-added lavender products including lotions, sprays, mists, creams, oils, soaps, lip balm, bath salts, candles, sachets, teas, herb mixes, and even lavender sugar—a very impressive array!

Their farm is a tourist destination by reservation only, so they also sell live plants, give seminars, conduct tours, and do consulting. The retired couple estimates that they make nearly half of their family income from those purple flowers.

They are so devoted to this plant that they traveled to France to learn how to grow it properly, and they think it makes a perfect plant on a microfarm because lavender is extremely easy to grow. As Elizabeth puts it, "Our fields are alive with the scent of lavender during July and August. The intense fragrance will leave you feeling as though you are at a lavender farm in Provence, France. There is nothing quite so wonderful as a field of lavender. The scent is intoxicating and pleasing to the senses."

The Inmans are microfarmers who work every angle they can to sell their products. They have a shopping cart on their website, work farmers' markets, particularly in Santa Fe, exhibit in festivals, supply wedding planners, have a retail store on their farm, and also sell their products wholesale to other retailers. To do all this, they have ten part-time day laborers who do most of the planting and harvesting. And they are steadily expanding their plantings and want to eventually fill all of their twelve acres with purple flowers.

Elizabeth's main advice to people who want to microfarm is to make sure to have multiple income streams as they do. And don't be tentative, be committed—make it your top goal to have a successful farm. Write a business plan and stick to it. If you love what you do, keep on doing it, she says, but don't neglect your community and your family. Keep learning, too. But don't try to do everything yourself—everyone needs a little help now and then.

A Microfarm Blossoms

Jennie Love grew up on a dairy farm but she's not passionate about cows. She prefers flowers ("they smell better"), and that's what she's growing now on her two-acre farm in Philadelphia she calls "Love 'n Fresh Flowers." She started the farm as a market garden after renting several plots from the Schuylkill Center Community Garden, then clearing them of invasive plants and building fences and gates to keep out the deer. And she won over some skeptical neighbors with—what else—bouquets of flowers. But the demand for her bouquets grew so fast she needed more space, and she found it from a friend, who leased her more land that was already fenced. So she built a hoop house on the new land where she starts seedlings and leads floral design workshops.

Jennie fully supports her family with the profits from her microfarm—she also grows some veggies to help out her kitchen. These profits are the result of the Community Supported Agriculture program she offers, where customers become members by signing up on her website, and they receive fresh flowers from May to September by picking them up at local retailers, mostly markets. Her philosophy is simple: "All bouquets are created exclusively with locally and organically grown flowers that were just harvested before showing up in the store. These bouquets are unlike any other you've ever purchased at a grocery store and typically last at least a week and often longer." She grows varieties that are not seen in shops, markets, and florists: Dianthus, Calendula, anemones, bachelor buttons, pink dahlias, strawflowers, purple asters, and zinnias.

As might be imagined, weddings are a large part of her business. Bouquets and displays are a natural for her, but her "value-added products" are rental items to make a wedding special, like tarnished antique silver, endearingly chipped and colorful vintage tins, rustic wooden boxes in all shapes and sizes, small vintage tables and dressers, and hand-painted signs for lawn games and directing guests.

Jennie does most of the farm work herself, but she has two part-timers during the height of the season to help her, and she said that it took a long time to find exactly the right people. One of the lessons she's learned is that a microfarmer must study her or his employees to learn how to use their skills efficiently. And she doesn't want to expand her flower farm, but rather grow the

flowers more efficiently. Another lesson she learned was that she had to master the wedding business, and there's a real learning curve for that.

For other microfarmers who might want a blooming farm, she says, pick high-value crops that will turn a big profit. "I can't make a profit growing lettuce," she points out. But other microfarmers might be able to with the right business plan.

Jennie Love of Love 'n Fresh Flowers.
Photo by Brooke Courtney, courtesy of Love 'n Fresh Flowers.

Chef Matt Yohalem of Il Piatto, Santa Fe, NM.
Photo by Doug Merriam, courtesy of www.burn-blog.com.

The Man Who Buys $120,000 of Local Produce a Year

All microfarmers need buyers, regardless of what they grow. In addition to market managers and retail purchasers, other buyers can be chefs and restaurateurs who really treasure locally grown foods. Meet Matt Yohalem of Il Piatto, Santa Fe's Italian Farmhouse Kitchen,

who's included in this book because he was the main chef I provided tomatoes and culinary herbs to during the 2013 season—and still do to a lesser extent from my greenhouse. In an interview with Matt over one of his unique and delicious lunches, he told me how he deals with microfarmers at farmers' markets and what he's looking for in a long-term business relationship with them. He's been buying locally produced foods since 1995, so he has a lot of experience in this business.

During the summer, he arrives at the market early, making his presence known and reserving any special items he realizes are going to sell out quickly. He asks the farmer to reserve a certain amount of produce for him to pick up later. Then he returns around noon to pick up the reserved vegetables and look for bargains from farmers who definitely do not want to take produce back to their farm. For example, a farmer may have some tomatoes that would not look particularly good in a salad, but would work well in a sauce, so Matt would make him an offer to buy all of them. The farmer by this time just wants to go home, so he'll usually take any reasonable offer.

I asked Matt what irritates him the most about farmers' markets, and he said that generally a lot of farmers treat the market as a social meeting place rather than a place to conduct business. Those who are busy chatting up their neighbors and not paying attention to customers won't make as many sales. Other irritations for Matt include farmers who show up at the market ill-equipped to do business—they have no scale, or no calculator, or no change, or no bags for the buying customers. He said that some farmers want to sit in the back of their booths eating out of a Taco Bell bag rather than stand in the front of the booth talking to customers. He urges farmers to dress well, stand up at all times, and avoid eating fast food when they're trying to sell organic lettuce, or whatever they're selling. Also, farmers should not try to sneak "foreign" crops into their booth—those that were not grown in the region.

His advice to microfarmers just getting started is to go to the markets as a customer and observe what is being sold and what is not. If three-quarters of the vendors are selling heirloom tomatoes, that might not be a crop to choose to grow. If very few farmers are selling heirloom eggplants, that crop might be a possibility. And they should always be thinking about unusual crops that might be missing from the market, like, say, decorative gourds or luffa sponges.

Most of the farmers at these markets would rather sell retail to the general public than sell wholesale to chefs because the profit is higher. So the farmers who wish to sell to chefs because of the security of long-term arrangements should avoid the markets and deal with chefs *by appointment only*. Farmers who show up at 11:45 at the restaurant's back door with boxes of produce won't get very far with Matt, or many other chefs, for that matter. They have to take care of their customers and don't have time to listen to sales pitches at lunch time.

The proper method to use with chefs is to make an appointment, show up on time, dress nicely, and bring the chef an appropriate gift, possibly something prepared from the produce you're trying to sell, like a raspberry jam, or a new, flavored goat cheese. Be imaginative. Would a chef rather receive a large, raw onion or a jarred pesto you made with your culinary herbs? Your next step is to bring up a recent menu and ask him about the ingredients he needs the most. Matt says that if some farmer asks him if he will buy five pounds of shallots a week, he turns around and asks the farmer, "Can you guarantee that you can supply them if I commit?" Farmers need to understand how important it is to fulfill the contracts they make with chefs, but here's a warning: the guarantees only go in one direction. This means that they only favor the buyer.

If the chef needs those shallots and you can't provide them like you promised, you'd better bite the bullet and go over to Whole Foods and buy some there rather than let the chef down. But if you show up with five pounds of shallots and the chef says, "Business has been lousy, so I only need two pounds this week," bite the bullet, sell him the two pounds, and tell him you hope business picks up. And remember, every single thing you provide to a chef should be clean. Even if it has a skin like an onion, wash and dry every single one of them. "But the chef's going to have his staff peel them, anyway," you protest. That's not the point. If you take pride in your produce, the chef will too.

Matt says that his most difficult suppliers to work with are the foragers. They collect mushrooms, piñon nuts, and huckleberries in the mountains around Santa Fe. According to Matt, the foragers are unpredictable amateurs who show up at the restaurant at any time during the day and usually over-value their mushrooms or other items by a factor of three or four times what they are worth. And the mushrooms are often not cleaned at all, just yanked out of the ground and thrown in a bag. He usually tells foragers to make the rounds to other restaurants and then come back with what they couldn't sell. Then he offers them a fair price for the rest of what they have.

He swears that he has no agenda about the farm to table movement—he's not trying to change the world by buying locally, or convince people to go organic or become vegetarians. "I buy locally grown food for one reason only," he told me. "It just tastes better!"

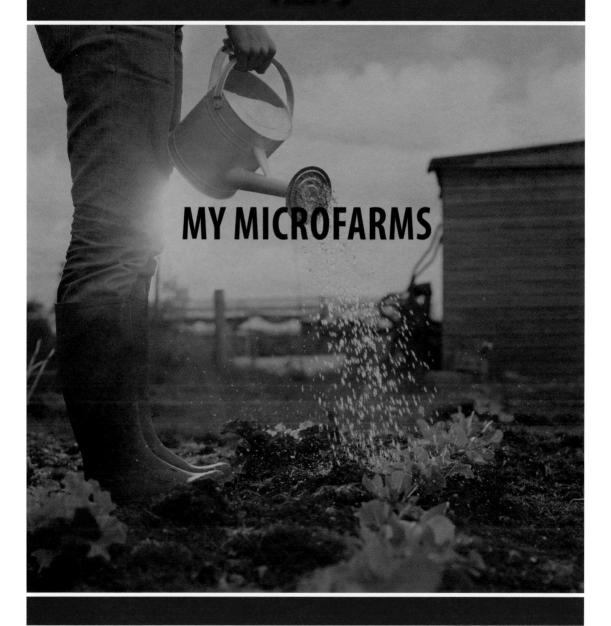

PART 3

MY MICROFARMS

I mentioned in the introduction that I had a microfarm when my wife at the time decided to open a retail plant boutique in the early 1970s. I supplied it with plants I grew in our ramshackle greenhouse. That was the legal one. About ten years after that, we had moved to New Mexico and I was persuaded by the same wife and a married couple who were friends of ours to create a second one, which was highly illegal. Since the statute of limitations has long since expired and with marijuana being legalized in various ways by 23 states plus the District of Columbia, I'm now comfortable telling the story in print for the first time. This section also takes you through the development and success of my current microfarms in Albuquerque and Las Cruces, New Mexico.

The Illegal Microfarm in a Barn

The deal was this. The couple were in the horse business, and my wife was enamored of horses, so they were more my wife's friends than mine. The couple—let's call them Joe and Linda—had an insurance settlement from a house fire and wanted to buy land and erect a structure to clandestinely grow marijuana and sell it wholesale. Of the four people involved, I was the only one who had actually grown it. Never on the scale that was planned, but even back then I knew how to grow many plants, and marijuana is an easy weed to grow. And profitable. If you don't get busted.

Setting Up the Deal

Their plan was to have a small horse ranch in a rural setting, so they would need a mobile home as a residence, an iron pipe corral, and a large metal prefab barn that would really be a greenhouse disguised as a barn. If anyone asked, Joe was going to tell them that it was a solar-heated foaling barn and a winter barn for the other horses at night.

The four of us visited a company that sold such barns and while Joe and Linda charmed the salesman, I took readings with a light meter and determined there would be plenty of light if we alternated metal and translucent panels on the roof and the south-facing side. By the end of the day we had placed a $2,000 deposit down on a 3,000 square foot metal and fiberglass barn.

Since I was responsible for both finding the necessary seeds and eventually selling the crop, my goal was to find one person who could take care of both of those needs. But I had to use caution because of the illegality of the operation—it was difficult to trust anyone in those days. I put the word out to a few trusted friends that I was going to grow a crop and needed seeds and then a buyer for the whole crop because I didn't want to be peddling grass by the ounce. After a few days, word came back that a long-time friend of mine had a connection he could introduce me to, and he would act as an intermediary.

Bedding plants in cans.
Photo by Dave DeWitt.

The initial planting.
Photo by Dave DeWitt.

Let's call the connection Robert, and he seemingly led a straight existence—short hair, a career in the finance segment, and even an office. But in reality he was a major importer of Mexican marijuana. Joe had urged me to operate with others on a need-to-know basis, so I was in the uncomfortable position of attempting to make a sale without giving up any information. At our initial meeting, Robert impressed me with his knowledge of the pot smuggling business, and he suggested that if I grew the crop from seeds he provided, he would buy the entire crop at the going wholesale rate, which ranged at the time

from $250 to $400 a pound. But he wanted the female flower tops to be seedless—*sinsemilla*. I would have to remove any male plants before they released pollen. I knew all about this from growing the stuff indoors under lights. Even the male leaves could be sold for a few bucks.

We struck a deal at that initial meeting, a $2,500 option to buy the entire crop, but Joe still had to approve it, since it was his land and barn-to-be, so I set up a meeting for the three of us. It did not go well, because Joe was a cowboy and Robert was a dope dealer, and in those days, those two groups did not get along, much less trust each other. But Joe did not blow up the deal, and the two seemed to put aside their differences for the sake of profit. On the drive back from the meeting, Joe told me he didn't like Robert, or trust him at all, and before taking his money and seeds, we should broaden our options.

"Okay, you find another buyer who's got seeds," I told him. "There's too much work to do to let worrying about our buyer hold us up. Are we a go or not?"

Joe had little choice in the matter, since he didn't have any connections, so he caved in. Robert promptly paid the option in cash, gave me the seeds, and never asked where we were growing them. Later, I found out why. We divided up the work: Joe, Linda, and my wife would stay on the ranch and help prepare the barn site, while I would be in Albuquerque working—that is, producing radio and TV commercials and germinating pot seeds.

On the property, Joe had a mobile home set up, built pipe corrals for the horses, had a well sunk, and electricity installed. He supervised the pouring of the footings for the barns in a blizzard while I was studying every book I could find on marijuana cultivation. The most useful book was *Marijuana Botany*, by Robert Connell Clarke, and it's still in print thirty-two years later. I had only grown the stuff indoors, so I was facing a totally unfamiliar growing scenario that was fraught with late frosts, different humidity, and soil composition.

A crew from the barn company erected our new, disguised greenhouse in about four days. The salesman dropped by during construction and asked if he could bring prospective buyers over to examine the barn—he told Joe he could sell dozens of solar-heated foaling barns. Joe was nice to him when he told him how much we

treasured our privacy. Meanwhile I was visiting all my favorite restaurants to collect forty-six-ounce metal cans that made perfect pots for pot seedlings.

Joe had been keeping track of the early morning temperatures inside the barn, and amazingly enough, it retained enough heat during the night to keep the inside temperature above freezing. It was time to move all my plants from the sunroom of Joe's rental house to the barn. There were two tense trips in a borrowed van (no windows) covering a distance of about 150 miles each way, but we kept to the speed limit and made it with no problems. Joe found a source for aged horse manure—we didn't have enough yet on the ranch—and we rototilled truckloads of it into the soil, then with shovels, cut rows and furrows exactly the way chile fields are built, and planted hundreds of young plants that averaged eight inches tall. Everything clicked on the project— light, heat, soil—and I knew that the pot farm would work. Then we ran out of money.

The First Crisis

A combination of factors brought on our first crisis in early May. The mobile home, well, footing, barn construction, and electrical had pushed our costs beyond $20,000, and we had to find survival cash to last us until the harvest. With everyone else working on the ranch and the growing project, the fundraising responsibilities fell to me. I borrowed money from credit cards and friends, which eased the crunch for a while.

In late June, we were broke again, but the good news was that the plants were growing phenomenally fast. It's unheard of today to sell leaf, or trim, in the current vernacular. In those days really good marijuana was so rare that you could sell the weak leaves after they had been

The maturing crop.
Photo by Dave DeWitt.

dried for about a third of what the tops brought. I decided to raise money by harvesting about a fourth of the most mature plants and sell the leaf to Robert. I had enough plants in metal pots left to replace them, so we wouldn't really be losing any time. We managed to scrape together about ten pounds of leaf, Robert liked it, and offered us $200 a pound. But I made several crucial mistakes in my first dope deal: I left too many large stems in each pound, I failed to eliminate the bright green color by curing the leaf, and I took a check from Robert. After all, the first one had cleared.

I cleared up the mess with Robert by adjusting the price, he paid in cash, and we moved on, but Joe had lost all faith in Robert and said that he was going to look for buyers out of state with a connection he had from college. I agreed, and it was a good thing he did that, as things turned out. The remainder of the summer growing season went by without incident, with the exception of a rogue male plant I missed at first that released some pollen before I removed it. There was a white fly breakout, but it was minor, and the female plants were starting to get large *sinsemilla* tops as the days got shorter. I had no idea how much weight-wise we were going to produce, but it would be a lot. Then everything went upside down.

The Second Crisis

While I was in Albuquerque, two men in pickups showed up at the ranch and caught Joe, Linda, and my wife working the horses in the corral. At gunpoint, they herded everyone to the mobile home, tied up my wife and friends, blindfolded them with bandanas, and proceeded to cut down all the plants in the barn. My wife and Linda managed to loosen the bandana over Joe's eyes, and as the pickups were driving away, Joe memorized the license plate number of one of them. A friend of Linda's worked at the Motor Vehicle Division and soon she had a name and address for the pickup.

I cannot go into details, but to make a very long story short, Joe and I tracked down one of the guys from the raid, and as Joe thought, Robert was responsible for it. I suspect that Robert had me followed one of the times I drove to the ranch from Albuquerque. To resolve the issue, let's just say that Joe tracked down Robert and persuaded him to take us to where the harvest was stashed. Most of the best tops were gone by the time we got there, but we did recover perhaps thirty percent of the harvest. Joe and I drove it to California, which was scary, but we ended up selling enough to Joe's new connection to cover a lot of our expenses. No one got hurt, and the police were not involved. We were very, very lucky. That was when I vowed that my marijuana microfarming days were over, and I've kept that vow. Instead, I chronicled the successful, one-year growing cycle of a first-time licensed medical marijuana grower in *Growing Medical Marijuana*. See Part 2 of this book for more details on Leo Lascaux.

The ultimate irony of the entire marijuana microfarm mashup was that both my wife and I and Joe and Linda divorced after the fiasco. Later, my now ex-wife married Joe. No, I was not best man at Joe's wedding. I've heard that the grow barn is, indeed, a real horse barn now, but I haven't heard anything about foals.

Objectively, using powerful hindsight, I was a complete idiot to undertake the grow barn. That said, I didn't have much personal risk. I didn't own the land or the barn. I only spent a small amount of time at the grow barn after it became illegal. There were no growing plants at my home. The law would have had to actually catch me on the premises to charge me with illegal cultivation, or, even more difficult, prove that I was part of a conspiracy to commit a felony. I mentioned this to a lawyer friend who told me it would have been a difficult case for the prosecution to prove me guilty of anything illegal. And it wasn't a total loss because I'm now writing about it! In fact, the money earned from the books about it have more than quintupled my original investment, proving that sometimes profits take a while to materialize.

Setting Up the 2013 Albuquerque Microfarm

My backyard microfarm consists of five elements: a greenhouse, a compost pile, two raised beds where I grow most of the plants, and a number of containers to grow the chiles that would be moved to a friend's large greenhouse before the first frost. I don't have enough room in my greenhouse to winter over thirty-four pots and still grow all the winter culinary herbs and greens for at least one restaurant.

The Greenhouse

More than twenty years ago, my wife, Mary Jane, and I got a loan to remodel our house, and part of that project was my ten-by-ten foot redwood greenhouse. I had built several flimsy greenhouses before, made out of two-by-fours, nails, and polyethylene sheeting for the roof and sides. They worked, but not well. The sheeting did not last long and suffered from wind and ultraviolet light damage, and they were impossible to efficiently heat in the winter. I knew I had to do this greenhouse the right way, which necessitated hiring a contractor, pouring a slab, choosing the right wood, and selecting the proper material for the roof and one side.

A contractor and I sketched it out and made a plan. A concrete slab would anchor it and one wall would be the west side of our house, between my office window and Mary Jane's office window. A glass door would allow me to monitor the temperature inside the greenhouse without resorting to expensive—and in my experience—unreliable remote electronic sensors.

I insisted that the contractor use redwood for the frame and the wood sheathing on north- and south-facing sides. It was twice as expensive but I wanted redwood because it resists just about everything that destroys wood except fire: rain, dry rot, and termites. The roof and slanting west side of the greenhouse were made of a translucent polycarbonate sheeting, also expensive, that was UV resistant and easier to use than rippled fiberglass. I had a small window installed on the west side and a high-mounted exhaust fan on the south side. It cost about $3,000 to build, but that included paying the contractor for his labor

The redwood greenhouse at my microfarm.
Photo by Don James.

since I'm an amateur carpenter at best. It was a marvelous investment, and I'm still using it with only minor repairs twenty years later.

Basically, we used the greenhouse to winter-over large tropical potted plants like thirty-five-year-old hibiscus plants in pots that I have to use a hand truck to move, as well as dwarf mangos, bougainvilleas, and other flowering plants. We also used it to start seeds in the winter and early spring. As I moved into microfarming more and more, I started giving away the tropicals to increase the space for starting more valuable plants. To that end, I decided to increase my greenhouse growing space by going vertical.

I built a series of shelves just wide enough to support medium-sized pots a gallon or less in volume along the south wall the greenhouse shares with the house, and across the west translucent wall. When I was done, I added up the square footage of the shelves and discovered that I had increased my growing space in the greenhouse by 20.5 percent.

Before I moved in, after Mary Jane and I married, she had planted a small male mulberry tree on the west side of the house, which grew large enough to completely shade the greenhouse during the summer. I paid a yard guy to cut down the tree and haul it away in 2012 because it was too close to the house, and without the tree, the winter light was increased because there were no tree branches or trunk to block the sun. Now, I could use the greenhouse during the summer — but not to grow anything. It was far too hot for that, so hot in fact that it became my new solar dryer. More on that later.

During the winter, I only need to heat the greenhouse at night; during the day, the solar gain keeps the greenhouse quite warm. Often, on a clear day when the outside temperature is about fifty, I have to open up the door and window of the greenhouse or it will get too hot in the afternoon. I always keep a five-gallon bucket of water in the greenhouse in case the hose from the outdoor faucet freezes, which it often does. Occasionally I will have white flies as a pest during the winter, but they are easily controlled with hanging, sticky flytraps. I'm fortunate that I've never had an outbreak of spider mites, which are, in my opinion, the worst type of greenhouse infestation.

At night I heat the greenhouse with an oil-filled, radiator-style, 1500-watt, Sunbeam space heater that I don't think is made any longer. But you can get another brand, like DeLonghi or Honeywell. They are the safest heaters to use in a greenhouse because there are no open heating elements that can start a fire, or short out if splashed with water. There is also no fan on this style of heater, but the metal fins diffuse the heat very well without any moving parts that can fail. Mostly I use the 800-watt setting and that keeps the temperature at night in the fifties. Only if the outside temperature drops below twenty degrees do I use the higher setting. I estimate the cost of electricity for heating the greenhouse at night in the winter to be less than $100 per year.

The Compost Pile

My father taught me about the value of composting when I was about eight, and so whenever I've had a garden, a compost pile is part of it. Some people are disgusted by rotting compost and the insects it attracts, but not me. Compost is just a necessary part of the garden cycle that will add nutrients and organic material to your growing medium. It is also a handy way to recycle garden and kitchen scraps and waste, and the result is a natural fertilizer and soil enhancement. Don't be put off by the idea of rotting vegetation and bad smells. A properly managed compost pile doesn't smell that bad at all. If yours smells bad, you're doing something wrong. I built two of them using wire screening and black plastic for less than $10.00.

Now I'm not going to take the time to teach you how to compost—most basic gardening books will cover that. Just remember that all compost should be vegetable material, not animal material. No meat or animal waste should ever be put in the pile. Leaves, grass clippings, garden waste, trimmings, and kitchen vegetable scraps all make good compost. Sticks and thick stems do not.

The First Raised Bed

I use raised beds for growing chiles and tomatoes because we live near the Rio Grande, and the soil here is part clay, part sand, with little organic material and a lot of salts, like calcium chloride. Raised beds allow me to add better soil and manure to the dirt in my backyard and better control my microfarm. My oldest raised bed was built with two-by-sixes, and it was long and narrow, twenty-eight feet by four feet, giving me 112 square feet growing space. But its shallow depth meant the roots were in both my prepared soil mix and below it into the yard soil. And since it's an enormous amount of work to replace all the soil mix each year, I just added steer manure and rototilled it in. I estimate the cost of the first bed at $50.00. I'm going to replace the two-by-sixes with railroad ties as described below, so I'll have more depth for better root development, which means larger, healthier plants. And using

raised beds makes crop rotation easier in your microfarm.

Because of space limitations, when you grow food crops on your microfarm, it's more difficult to rotate your crops each year. In southern New Mexico, farmers commonly rotate the main crops, chile peppers, cotton, and alfalfa, with the last crop, fixing nitrogen in the soil as a natural fertilizer enhancement. But microfarmers can't make any money growing cotton or alfalfa, so their options are reduced. I say, don't worry about it all that much. The real soil depleters are crops you probably won't be growing, like wheat, corn, or silage. Raised beds—rather that just one large area—make it easier to keep track of which crops are grown where.

Building the New Bed

Instead of using boards and nails, I smartened up for my new bed and bought eight non-organic, creosote-treated railroad ties, nine feet long and one foot wide. I laid four in a square, with the ends abutting, then laid four more ties on top of those. That was it. It took two of us less than a half hour to build it and it cost about $125, which included a delivery fee. The abutting ends caused a loss of one foot on each of the four sides, so I ended up with sixty-four square feet of growing space, a little more than half the size of my first bed. But the bed would be twice as deep.

The next step was to fill up a rather large space, about sixty-four cubic feet (since the depth was just a foot, the square and cubit feet shared the same digit), with a growing medium. I used a mix of about two-thirds commercial bagged "top soil," which is composed of milled sphagnum moss and other organic materials, and about one-

Tomatoes and superhot chiles in a raised bed.
Photo by Dave DeWitt.

third bagged aged steer manure, plus a few cubic feet of compost from my pile that had aged for two years. I layered the bed as much as possible by alternating the bags of soil and manure, plus the compost. When I was done, my nephew Max brought his rototiller over and mixed it thoroughly.

Then I bought the Green Thumb brand flat weeper or soaker hoses and ran them in lines spaced about a foot apart, covering the entire top of the bed. The connector to the main garden hose ran through a corner space between the railroad ties. Then I covered the hoses with a garden fabric, but you can use a landscaping fabric too, as long as it's porous. I fastened it down by stapling it to the edges of the railroad

ties. Those ties will still be in place in the twenty-third century. Creosote and dry air? That means forever.

The second bed was ready for planting, but I still wanted my other main crop to have some mobility. And that crop would be superhot peppers. Since Marlin Bensinger and I had a three-quarter acre field with five thousand of these plants started in Las Cruces already (see below), my goal was to see if I could grow a reasonable yield of a superhot variety, namely 'Barrackapore,' in the Zone 6 climate of Albuquerque, two hundred miles further north. I would grow the seedlings in the new bed beside the tomatoes, and in pots.

Superhots in containers.
Photo by Dave DeWitt.

The Containers

My friend Kathi Caldwell, who owns a South Valley greenhouse operation and who germinated the plants for our Las Cruces field, described below, loaned me thirty-four five-gallon, black, tough plastic nursery pots that had great drainage. Now, what growing medium to use? In raised beds, the drainage is always great because the excess water will flow through the spaces in the uneven railroad ties, so always adding roughage—manure, compost—will not impede the water flow. But in a pot, the same mix of top soil, manure, and compost compacts too much in the narrow space and tends to restrict the plants' roots.

So I bought perlite from a greenhouse supply store. Perlite is a natural, though inorganic, spacer in the pots, and is rather expensive for the microfarmer when purchased from the big box house and garden stores. These places wanted $9.00 to $13.00 for eight quarts of perlite, which is way too expensive for relatively large-scale growing. I needed a wholesale source, but they don't sell to the general public. I drove to Greenhouse and Garden Supply and tried to buy some.

"I'm sorry," said the clerk, whose name tag read "Mysti," "but we don't sell to the general public. Businesses only."

"I have a farm," I told her. "Do I qualify?"

"Yes. We sell wholesale to farmers and retailers. What's the name of your farm?"

Oops. My farm didn't have a name yet. I had a corporation called Sunbelt Shows, but producing shows had nothing to do with farming. Then it came to me.

"It's new," I said, "starting this year. Sunbelt Microfarm." She entered the name into the computer and, just like that, I had a commercial account. I bought six cubic feet of perlite for $21.23. That's 180 quarts, by the way, so for twice the money, I received 22.5 times the amount of perlite. And my microfarm suddenly had a name. I felt that the entire project was now very real and official.

The formula I used for the soil was 7/8 bagged top soil to 1/8 perlite, and I thoroughly mixed this together in the garden cart before shoveling the mix into the pots. With the beds and containers ready, it was time for the plants.

If it has a logo, it must be official.
Sunbelt Microfarms logo courtesy of Sunbelt Media.

Starting the Seedlings

I was facing a bit of a dilemma when it came to choosing which varieties of tomatoes to grow. I wanted to grow heirloom varieties of tomatoes rather than hybrids because I thought they'd be worth more. The heirlooms were a bit more susceptible to disease and they produced fewer fruits, but I thought a sign reading "organic, heirloom tomatoes" would increase their value. But that was months before I studied the tomato prices at the growers' market in the downtown park. I focused on three varieties that had been successful for me in the past: 'Brandywine,' 'Cherokee Purple,' and 'Mortgage Lifter.' I planted the seeds in trays over the Christmas holidays and the germination was good (about eighty percent) and the seedlings grew well, with no diseases like damping-off (I kept a fan going constantly) or insect damage.

The superhot chiles were more problematic. I had two varieties, the 'Barrackapores' from plants we had previously grown in Las Cruces, and another that was called 'Primo Scorpion' that was developed by Troy Primeaux and his friends at the University of Louisiana in Lafayette. I treated the seeds by soaking them first in a mild bleach solution and then planted them in trays placed on heating pads in the greenhouse. Germination was lousy, about forty percent, and the plants that did sprout grew so slowly that I began to worry that some of them would not be large enough to transplant when May came around. So I began to fertilize them with a mild solution of 20-20-20 water fertilizer and they started doing better. Superhot peppers seem to need more nitrogen than other varieties like, for example, 'NuMex 6-4,' for some as yet unknown reason. Finally, the seedlings were large enough to transplant to two-inch pots, where they would stay until they were moved into the beds and pots. Still, they were the slowest-growing chiles I've ever planted. It was frustrating.

Planting the Beds and Pots

In the original bed, I planted about one-third of the tomatoes in three-fourths of the bed. In the remaining space, I planted broccoli, chard, and kale for home use. Two-thirds of the tomatoes and about half of the chiles went into the new bed, with the remaining chiles in the pots. It was the first week in May, a few days past the average date of the last frost in the South Valley, traditionally May first. I thought I was home free. I was wrong.

Two nights later, a cold front passed through, dropping the temperatures to thirty or thirty-one degrees, depending on what part of the valley you lived in. The frost got all of the flowering fruit trees in the orchards next to my typical hike down near the Rio Grande, with the exception of a couple of apple and pear trees. It also wiped out a third of my chiles and tomatoes. It could have been much worse except for the vagaries of frost and the way it moves according to breezes.

Fortunately, I had a backup plan. Sort of. I had kept some of the smaller tomato and chile seedlings in small pots in the greenhouse. I had enough tomatoes but was short on the chiles. A quick trip to Kathi's greenhouse solved the chile problem and I was back in business. Until the leafhoppers struck three weeks later, that is.

Leafhoppers and Curly Top

Curly top is a viral disease that resides in two of New Mexico's most common weeds, Russian thistle (tumbleweeds) and London rocket (a type of mustard). It is spread by the beet leafhopper, which sucks virus-laden sap from the infected weed and carries it to beets, tomatoes, peppers, beans, potatoes, spinach, and squash. I have seen entire chile fields destroyed by curly top because there is no known remedy for it. Farmers spray insecticides to try to kill the leafhoppers but that is almost always ineffectual because of the sheer number of insects. In a home garden or microfarm, entomologists suggest caging your plants with fine netting to create a physical barrier, but that is a very time-consuming and somewhat expensive proposition, especially considering the size of some full-grown tomato plants. What happens to the cage when the plant is six feet tall and four feet wide?

Entomologists have not completely figured out the life cycle of the leafhoppers. Some of them claim that leafhoppers migrate north (they fly as well as hop) and once they're gone, the danger is over (not!), or that companion planting of marigolds to supposedly repel them, and petunias and geraniums that "trap" them will solve the problem. I've tried companion planting and it is only of marginal effectiveness and takes valuable space out of the growing area. I have noticed though, as spring turns into summer, the danger of leafhoppers diminishes. My theory is not that they're migrating out of New Mexico, but rather that they are endemic and their life cycle is over for the year. I think that the severity of leafhoppers and the virus they spread is directly related to the amount of spring moisture a given area receives. If spring is wet, curly top will be a problem; if dry, not so much of one.

Right before the leafhoppers dropped by for a visit, I counted my plants and discovered that I had fifty-eight tomato plants and sixty-two superhot chiles. The tomatoes were growing like crazy and the superhots were just moseying along, which I have now learned is their typical lazy tropical way because, down in Trinidad where they originated, it's summer year-round, so why hurry?

One after another, some of the tomatoes stopped growing and the leaves started curling in toward their centers. I knew they were infected, so I yanked them out of the garden and threw them in the trash. But I had no seedlings left to replace them, so I was off to the nurseries and even big box stores to see what they had left in the middle of June. Hybrids, of course: 'Early Girl,' 'Big Boy,' 'Better Boy,' and all the usual suspects produced mostly by

the mega-greenhouses of Bonnie Plants. I had no option but to buy them. I didn't keep count, but I replaced between one-third and half of the heirlooms. I estimate the cost of the replacement plants at about $40. This was about half of what the original plants had cost.

Interestingly, only one superhot chile plant was affected, and I wasn't even sure what disease that plant had. The leaves didn't curl, but the pods turned yellow instead of red, fell on the mulch, and rotted. I removed the poor thing from the bed and threw it and the rest of its pods away.

About two weeks after replacing tomatoes for the second time, some of the survivors had tomatoes that were showing a color other than pale green. The harvest had begun.

A wall of tomatoes.
Photo by Dave DeWitt.

Tomatoes being sundried in the greenhouse.
Photo by Dave DeWitt.

The Tomato Processor: Me

I was finishing up another book around this time, *Dishing Up New Mexico*, a project that put me in touch with the New Mexico microfarmers, as well as product manufacturers and chefs. One of those chefs was Matt Yohalem (see Part 2), who was the owner and executive chef of Il Piatto in Santa Fe, which he describes as New Mexico's Italian Farmhouse Kitchen. I had met him once before and he had submitted five recipes for that book, and the recipes impressed me. He was a true farm to table chef, creating all his menus from locally grown produce, meats, and dairy, and he resisted buying from food service suppliers as much as he could.

Meanwhile, although my total June harvest was a meager half-pound, by mid-July a typical day was producing a couple of pounds, so I had to decide what to do with them. I knew that Matt must go through hundreds of pounds of tomatoes

a month, so I started washing and pureeing them in my blender. I called him up, made an appointment, and met him at the restaurant with a cooler full of tomato puree in freezer bags and about ten zip storage bags of culinary herbs: basil, sage, oregano, thyme, and Italian parsley.

Matt was impressed with my harvest so far, and he said that all the puree I had brought him would last at most a couple of days. But that was okay, and he asked how much yellow puree I could make, and I replied not much because I hadn't planned for it. He said his customers would love a yellow tomato sauce used as some clever garnish for a side dish, and I mentioned that there were other tomato colors too, such as orange and chocolate from a variety called 'Chocolate Cherry' and that I could grow them during the 2014 season. Matt asked if I could provide herbs during the winter, and I told him yes, I could, by growing them in my greenhouse. Then he asked a question that surprised me.

The ripening table I used for tomatoes and peppers.
Photo by Dave DeWitt.

"Could you help me write a book about my restaurant?"

Next came a discussion about how we could work together. He had no uses for superhot peppers, but if he accepted all the tomatoes and culinary herbs I could grow, I would be one of his supplying farms, and thus I could be a part of the book he wanted to write about Il Piatto. In turn, he would be in two of my books, including the one you're reading now. His compensation would not only be my produce, but my knowledge of writing and book publishing. My compensation would be a percentage of the advance and royalties he earned from his book. When my produce was used in a dish, I would also be featured on his daily menu as a supplier. This was an arrangement that was similar to the one I had with Marlin Bensinger for the Las Cruces superhot field—I would be paid from the sales that my experience and connections could generate. I said yes and we had a deal. I had just learned that microfarmers need to have an open mind and be very flexible. During that meeting,

Matt had one last question.

"Can you sun-dry some of those tomatoes for me?"

By October thirteenth the microfarm had endured two light frosts that had blackened the tops of some of the tomato plants, but the fruits were undamaged. At that point in time, it was mild again and there were plenty of good-sized tomatoes on the plants, so the slow October harvest continued. So far, the harvest had generated 275.5 pounds. Could it possibly hit 300 before the first killing frost?

Meanwhile, Marlin Bensinger and I were in our third year of growing a one-acre superhot chile microfarm in Las Cruces, and that story dovetails with my Albuquerque microfarm.

The Las Cruces Superhot Farm

Marlin Bensinger and I tried and tried to come up with a joint moneymaking project for about twenty years, but nothing ever fell into place. We would meet annually at the New Mexico Chile Conference in Las Cruces and talk about it and vow that "Some day...." But he had his business doing lab tests and consulting on the building of oleoresin extraction plants for all kinds of essential oils, but particularly chile peppers. This was because more and more food manufacturers were discovering how well this oleoresin worked in food manufacturing. It was costly, but it went a long way in adding a specifically measurable heat to, say, potato chips. So Marlin brokered oleoresin capsicum as well with his company, Chromtec. And still does.

I was busy producing shows and writing books, so it seemed unlikely that we would ever find a project. Then superhot chiles came along. For me, they were a new chapter in the ever-

The Las Cruces superhot field.
Photo by Dave DeWitt.

evolving, ongoing popularity of chile peppers and fiery foods. For Marlin, they could supply a demand on all levels, from farming them and selling the fresh pods to making products as different as oleoresin and pickled pods. Our partnership arrangement was simple. Marlin would supply the start-up money and labor for a small field of just under one acre of superhot chiles. It would be my job to sell all the harvested pods through my connections in the chile pepper and fiery foods industries. For that, I would receive ten percent of the net profit. But since the field would be in Las Cruces with its longer growing season, and since the pods would be shipped from there, I wouldn't have to lift a shovel or touch a pod. I could do all the marketing of the pods through mass emails to my eight thousand contacts and banner ads on my four websites.

Marlin had some connections to greenhouse growers in Las Cruces who could germinate the seeds we had collected from a number of sources, and he contracted with them to begin germination in early January. Meanwhile, he leased the land and contracted with a farmer who had a tractor. Call this one a mechanized microfarm! The only thing he forgot to do was ask what had been previously grown on the land he leased. This was in 2011, and Marlin had good luck with his first microfarm. Together with his personal partner, Gillie Augeri, and some local helpers, all the seedlings that germinated in the greenhouse were put in the field in early April, and they included the varieties 'Trinidad Scorpion,' '7-Pot,' 'Chocolate Habanero,' and 'Bhut Jolokia.'

It was one of those growing seasons that only happens occasionally, to delight the farmer or gardener. Nothing went wrong. There was plenty of water. There was no curly top virus or Phytophthora root rot. Insects were no big deal, and weeds were under control. The plan was working and the plants were growing. Tall, very tall, some at more than five feet, large for most chiles and gigantic for superhots. When I saw them in all their glory, I said to Marlin, "Ten to one last year this was an alfalfa field." He made a call on his cell phone, then turned to me. "You're right."

Alfalfa fixes nitrogen in the soil and sometimes, when chile plants get too much of that element, they won't flower and fruit but continue vegetative growth and get quite large. But this was not the case here. The huge bushes were loaded with fruit, and soon harvesting commenced. That was successful too, and so were sales. My emails had produced all the leads we needed to sell the entire crop at premium prices for chiles, averaging $16.00 a pound. Compare that to growing New Mexican green chile, which was only earning the farmer about a dollar per pound at the field that year.

Most farmers would not complain about netting $16,000 on one acre during their first year of growing. But Marlin wanted to expand the field, even though the seed supply for superhots is iffy at best. He had saved seeds from the first year, but maybe not enough, and to add to the situation, he would have to deal with another land owner/farmer, and the growing project was getting a lot more complicated. Still, he more than doubled the size of the first field, and a one acre superhot field became a three and a half acre one. Marlin didn't foresee it, of course, but 2012 became one of those growing seasons that happens only occasionally to discourage the farmer or gardener. *Everything* went wrong.

Our greenhouse operator had lost a key employee, the woman in charge of germinating our crop. Her replacement failed to water our little seedlings, and they withered and died. More seeds were planted, but the garden was already six weeks behind schedule. It got worse. When the new seedlings were finally planted, they were very small and strong winds took out many of them. Then it was time for Marlin and Gillie to leave for their other home in Florida. By the time they returned two months later, when Marlin looked at the field he couldn't see the chile plants. They were covered by weeds. His workers had dropped the ball while he was gone.

So Marlin formulated a plan to save the field. The first step was finding the chiles, then cutting down all the weeds. So he and the workers *really* started working, and chopping weeds in the hot sun is hard, exhausting work, which is precisely why farmers and gardeners must not let the weeds get established in the first place. They uncovered as many chile plants as they could, and weeding the three and a half acres took six long weeks. It was a patchy field, harvest was low, and the 2012 growing season ended in a dead loss. Gardeners have failures quite often, but they just shrug off a failed crop or an outbreak of curly top that wipes out all the tomatoes—but microfarmers are trying to make money. We were. Win one, lose one, we thought, and Marlin was determined to do it right the next time.

In 2013, Marlin, the ever-organized scientist and engineer, and I reformulated the whole microfarm plan. Most of this was his work, but I supplied a valuable resource—Kathi Caldwell of Rio Valley Greenhouses in the South Valley,

which was pretty close to our house. She had experience germinating chile seeds, and growers in remote northern New Mexico areas loved her when she pulled up in her truck up loaded with chile pepper bedding plants. She had the space and she had the time to do all our germination. Plus, I could inspect it whenever I wanted. A deal was made and we were back in business. Kathi would germinate all of our seeds for $685.00.

With that problem solved, Marlin focused on the field and the application of water and nutrients. Water was especially critical because of the drought—there would be water running in Las Cruces irrigation ditches only once during the entire season. First, Marlin reduced the size of the field to three-quarters of an acre. Next, rows

Water and nutrient tanks.
Photo by Dave DeWitt.

and furrows were cut, and Marlin and the helpers laid drip lines just under the soil on top of the rows, placing an emitter every eighteen inches. Each row had its own valve, so the rows must be irrigated individually. Marlin installed three tanks with a total volume of about a thousand gallons. Before irrigating, he would add an enzyme solution with micronutrients to the water, along with nitric acid, which would neutralize the alkaline soil and bring the pH back close to a neutral. The cost of the irrigation system, which was a capital improvement rather than a growing cost that year, was $2,000, but Marlin was in it for the long haul.

Next he added fertilizer. One gallon of water-soluble 12-8-33 fertilizer was diluted with 220 gallons of water in the big tank along with the micronutrients. Next, Marlin added a series of three filters that would clean the water before it went into the drip system. A 140-micron mesh filter came first, which would remove any

solids that could have come up from the well. A 75-micron filter came next, followed by a 25-micron one. Thus Marlin could rest assured that no drip lines would clog. Fertilizer cost for the 2013 season was $787.00.

When the seedlings in Kathi's greenhouse were large enough to plant, Marlin drove up from Las Cruces with a trailer, and drove the plants back to the microfarm. Marlin, Gillie, and the workers carefully hand-planted them all. The irrigation system worked perfectly and the entire field could be drip-irrigated in just forty minutes. Constant weeding kept the field clear. There was no curly top virus in the field, and to my knowledge, no drip-irrigated field has ever had a case of Phytophthora because it is not water-saturated in the slightest. The plants were strong enough to tolerate the last of the spring winds. Marlin was weeks ahead of schedule, and the late frost that hit us up in Albuquerque did not dip 210 miles down to Las Cruces, so the plants were fine and grew faster than normal. But there were serious insect infestations.

Aphids and spider mites had fled the sprayed pecan trees and settled amongst our superhots. Marlin sprayed the field with FDA-approved insecticides. Sevin and malathion took care of them very well. We also had an outbreak of

Marlin Bensinger in his HPLC lab in Las Cruces.
Photo by Gilberta Augeri.

thrips, but that, too, was easily controlled. The insecticide and sprayer costs were $135.00. Chemicals, you ask? What about organic?

As mentioned once before, we'd love to grow everything organically. But our field is surrounded by pecan groves, onion fields, and alfalfa. This a perfect breeding ground for pests of all kinds. Our farmer neighbors around us spray when necessary, killing many of whatever is the pest of the month, and driving the rest of them away to a perfect, spray-free field, namely ours. If we didn't spray insecticides, our field would be decimated within a week. This is why organic doesn't work in the Las Cruces field but does in my backyard, where the bad insect population is a fraction of what it is in a farming community.

On October twenty-first, Marlin emailed me: "Harvest here will probably be less than 500 lbs. providing we get some additional growing time. Because of multiple infestations of aphids, spider mites, and thrips, what started out great turned into blossom drop and almost lost the whole field. I'm truly disappointed in the return on effort this year." Things were not looking good down south.

Cropover

I picked up the word "cropover" in Barbados, which essentially is their carnival-style harvest festival. In colonial days, Cropover celebrated the end of the sugarcane field work for the season, with the cane cut, the fields burned, the juice extracted from the canes, and then refined into molasses for shipping to New England's rum industry. For me, it meant no more daily watering, monitoring the plants, and picking fruits. Now all I had to do was take care of the wintered-over superhot plants in my greenhouse, plus grow culinary herbs for Il Piatto in Santa Fe.

This would amount to one-tenth of my daily farm work in the summer, or maybe even less.

I kept a handwritten daily harvest log of my tomatoes and the products I made from them, and the superhot chile pods, which I froze. The harvest started to wind down at the end of September, with both the chiles and the tomatoes taking much longer to ripen in the cooler weather. On October fifth and sixth, we had a mild frost, which blackened the tops of some of the tomato and chile plants, but the weather bounced back and I had to resume irrigating. Maybe I had some more time, since typically in the South Valley, the first killing frost happens in the third or fourth week in October. As it turned out, there were only ten more days of growing left.

The kill date for the outside microfarm was October seventeenth at about five o'clock in the morning when the temperature dropped to twenty-nine degrees, and the growing season was over. But the harvesting season was not. Although I did not reach three hundred pounds of tomatoes before the killing frost, there were still plenty of green tomatoes on the now-dead bushes. So I harvested about twenty or so pounds of greenies, put them in closed cardboard boxes in the greenhouse, and tried the old ethylene gas ripening treatment. That is the gas that ripening fruits of all kinds emit, from bananas to apples to tomatoes. Undoubtedly, some of the lighter-colored green tomatoes had started to ripen and maybe their gas would trigger ripening in the really green tomatoes, and the increased heat in the greenhouse—often ninety degrees when it was sixty outside—would hasten the ripening. I decided only to count the weight of those that ripened, since green tomatoes don't have much use and don't preserve well unless you make a relish, and you can only eat so much green tomato relish.

The tomato harvest statistics revealed a warped bell curve:

June: 0.5 pounds

July: 40.8 pounds

August: 146.6 pounds

September: 64.85 pounds

October: 57.80 pounds

On October thirty-first, the total tomato weight hit 310.55 pounds. And all the greenies that would ripen already had, so I put the remaining ones in the compost pile. The harvest of outside crops was over.

After the first frost, I kept seven of the smallest potted superhot chile plants, some of which had not even fruited yet, and took the remaining twenty-seven plants over to Kathi's greenhouse. She and I moved them into the sunniest place in her sunniest greenhouse. There were 110 pods on the plants, which I included in the total count. My chile plants in the center raised bed stopped flowering and started dropping leaves as they succumbed to the colder temperatures; in my warm greenhouse, they retained their leaves and continued to flower and set fruit. By the end of the season, my pod count finalized at 781 pods, or approximately thirteen pounds of superhots.

Marlin's Report on the Acre of Superhots

"It was like pushing a forty-foot chain," Marlin said, describing the microfarm. We were having beers at Farley's in late November, just before they left for Florida. Farley's is my favorite hangout in Las Cruces, partly because of their

sign that reads, "Sorry, We're Open." Gillie had joined us and the meeting was mostly to figure out what to do with the farm in 2014.

"It started in the greenhouse with snails mowing down the just-sprouted chile plants, and the ants bringing aphids, which we didn't notice when we planted the larger seedlings."

"And the lack of irrigation water," I pointed out.

"Yeah, just one flood irrigation the entire summer. And the heat just overwhelmed the drip system, which we should have put deeper into the rows."

"Or make flatter rows, like Lorenzo did." Lorenzo was an organic microfarmer near our house—see Part 2.

"Right. Then when the pecan and onion growers sprayed for spider mites and thrips, the little bastards took a vacation in our field."

"The amount of insecticide we had to use on that field was obscene," said Gillie.

"So, a profit only in one out of three years," I said.

"Right. But this year we did make some progress, and at least had a couple of hundred pounds to sell."

"And Lorenzo had 150 pounds from three short rows," I pointed out.

Marlin nodded. "And his neighbors in the South Valley of Albuquerque weren't growing pecans or onions. But the most annoying thing was that we had customers waiting for superhots they never got. And they were all different customers from the first year."

"Interesting," I said.

"We lost all the first year customers with the crop failure last year."

"But it means there's a lot of customers out there."

Ripening superhots.
Photo by Dave DeWitt.

"Yes," Marlin said. "More than we ever imagined."

"We could use all contract growers up in Albuquerque," I suggested.

"But Marlin installed the water tanks and the drip system at our field," Gillie pointed out.

"Move 'em," I replied.

"We've got a few months to figure this out," Marlin said, ordering another round of beers. Our farm meeting was over.

The bottom line was that Lorenzo and I had good crops, and we both planned to expand our superhot production. Marlin's part of it was still up in the air.

The Dynamics of Two Microfarms at Once

The microfarm in my backyard is more akin to gardening, while the one in Las Cruces more like real farming, with a tractor, rows and furrows, real drip irrigation instead of soaker hoses. My closely planted tomatoes weaving their stalks together into a wall of vines and fruit that I had to penetrate with my eyes and arms to harvest, contrasted with the neat, clean rows of superhot peppers in the manicured Las Cruces field. Yet both microfarms were harvested in the same manner, with human beings, not machines, picking by hand the tender, ripening fruits as they revealed their first hints of colors other than green. In both pepper pods and tomatoes, once the ripening has begun, it continues regardless of whether or not the fruit is on the vine. In fact, the plants, in their never-ending drive to reproduce more of their own kind, would rather be without those ripening fruits, and by removing them early, we give the plants the ability to keep flowering to produce more tomatoes or chiles loaded with their genetic signatures embedded in the seeds.

The Future of Sunbelt Microfarm

After the modest success of the 2013 microfarm, I was unsure whether or not I wanted to continue the project. On one hand, it was a lot of hard work and I didn't make much money on it. Then again, it was a start-up, and a fairly successful one. Plus I made a lot of good contacts. On the other hand, to continue meant expansion and even more work in 2014. I didn't need the money, either—in fact, I made much more money writing this book than I did growing all the stuff that I wrote about. I was very nearly going to end this book by announcing that the project was

over, the book was complete, and I only wanted to write more books and go back to being a simple gardener.

But then my friend Ethan Diness commented over lunch how much he had enjoyed growing the ornamental chiles for me from seeds sent from Italy by famed ornamental chile breeder Mario Dadomo of Parma, and that gave me pause for thought. Here's the back story on that little project. I'd known Mario for a few years after meeting him at the agricultural experiment station he worked at in Parma, and I'd shot photos of the mature ornamentals in his field. He and his wife, Manuela, had invited Mary Jane and I for lunch and then treated us to Italian deli specialties of many meats, cheeses, and the unbelievable aged *lardo*, which is fine lard seasoned with various herbs and kept in a cave for a few years. It was a wonderful feast and the start of a friendship of sorts—being long-distance most of the time, communication was limited to email.

Then in the spring of 2013 Mario emailed me and wanted to know if the seeds he produced could be marketed in the U.S. and was I interested? I said I was and he agreed to send me seeds for his favorite ornamentals—and he did. But I couldn't grow them in my yard for fear of them crossing with the superhots and ruining the resulting seeds. They would create hybrids with only a fraction of the heat. Then I thought of Ethan and his nice backyard.

Ethan is a friend of mine who was stuck in a low-paying job in the Culinary Arts department of Central New Mexico Community College, and he was tired of it. As a part-time caterer too, he much preferred being an entrepreneur, but was worried about paying the bills if he left a secure, if inadequate, job. On the other hand, he was extremely well-connected into the restaurant community of Albuquerque and knew a hell of a lot more chefs and restaurant owners than I did. He agreed to grow Mario's ornamentals and he would help me market superhots. Together, we prepared the bed for Mario's favorite varieties. Although we started late in the season, the ornamentals grew fast and I knew we would have a nice harvest to tell Mario about.

But then Mario suddenly died. It was what people call a massive stroke, and there was some email chatter for a week that he was speaking and actually might recover, but that didn't happen and Mario passed a few days later. I was stunned and saddened by my friend's sudden death.

I sent our sympathies to Manuela but I knew the ornamental seed marketing project was over. We did have a small but nice crop of beautiful, ornamental chiles in colors ranging from yellow to orange to red to purple. While looking at them, Ethan made his comment about enjoying growing them and it suddenly occurred to me that Ethan would make a great microfarming partner. He could fill in for me in the Valley when I was on a business trip and I could cover for him. With his help, I *could* expand my microfarm, both in volume and in crops grown. Looking at the multi-colored ornamental chiles, I recalled the first

time I had taken frozen tomato puree and fresh culinary herbs up to Matt Yohalem at Il Piatto. My lunch plate came garnished with a couple of sprigs of the blooming thyme I had brought.

"A couple of those ornamentals would make a beautiful garnish on a plate," I told Ethan.

"I could pickle them," Ethan suggested. "And then the chef could use them as needed."

Sometimes, partnerships happen quickly and simply.

A test bottle of superhot sauce, research for a value-added product. Photo by Dave DeWitt.

Winterwork

We based our business plan on what I had learned while writing this book and what was immediate reality for our partnership. We would have two microfarms, mine and Ethan's, so we changed our name to the plural Sunbelt Microfarms. That would also allow a possible expansion into the distribution of specialty crops grown on other local microfarms. We would base our income around high-value crops and high-end, value-added products, and first we would focus on supplying chefs who cooked with locally grown produce.

Our plan included raising specialty tomatoes and chile peppers, the usual culinary herbs and greens, and exotic mushrooms that would grow in part of the workshop at Ethan's house. We would build an additional raised bed in my backyard and install two or three of them in Ethan's backyard. The exotic chiles would be ornamentals and superhots, which we intended to pickle in twelve-ounce jars as one of our value-added products. The tomatoes would include the particularly colorful ones requested by Matt Yohalem: 'Kellogg's Breakfast Organic' (orange), 'Sunny Boy' (yellow), 'Chocolate Cherry' (brown/purple); these would be sun-dried for use in making exotic-looking garnish sauces for plated meals. Other tomatoes would include various large, red varieties that would also be sun-dried, but in addition, some of them would be roasted, peeled, left whole, and frozen in containers.

The culinary herbs and microgreens would be sold fresh to chefs who had previously alerted us to let them know what we had ready for use. A delivery system would have to be worked out, of course. We planned on experimenting with fresh pestos as a value-added product designed for chefs who were prep-chef challenged—in other words, they did not have the time or manpower to make such specialties as pestos.

The chile peppers in our microfarms would be superhots and ornamentals. The superhots would be pickled and we'd retail as many as we could to foodies attending the Fiery Foods Show, then sell the rest wholesale to hot shops. The ornamentals, varying in color and shape, would also be pickled and sold exclusively to chefs as a garnish for spicy dishes—sort of a visual warning sign.

Since there were only one or two independent mushroom suppliers in New Mexico, and they specialized in oyster mushrooms, we decided to attempt to grow shiitakes, creminis, black trumpets, and portabellas. Neither one of us had ever grown them, but it seemed like a pretty straightforward project to us. Climate modification in New Mexico's dry air would be a necessity for a successful crop, but mushrooms tend to grow quickly; from placing the mycelium (vegetative part) on the substrate (growing medium) to harvest is usually about six weeks for most varieties. It was worth a shot.

We also brainstormed some other ways to make money:
—Custom growing of specialty products for chefs.
—Brokering produce we don't grow; we could become a source that chefs can go to when they need something. We network with Lorenzo, who knows all the growers.
—Develop additional value-added products. Meanwhile, in my greenhouse, the herbs were growing well, and I delivered my first bunches of them to Matt on December twelfth along with Ethan, who gave Matt a jar of pickled ornamentals.

We were going to be all set up for spring planting. But if you're reading this book and thinking about becoming a microfarmer for the first time, you might not have everything ready to go. In that case, the next part of this book should be useful to you.

Report on the 2014 Superhot Microfarms

At the end of the 2013 season, Marlin, Gillie, and I were in a dead loss after three years of growing in basically the same field in Las Cruces. So we met for dinner when I was visiting, and reviewed the situation. Marlin pointed out that our contract grower, Lorenzo Candelaria, had produced about the same yield of pods from his 600 plants that we had *from our entire field* that started with 5,000 plants. I suggested that we find a bunch of Lorenzos and give them the starter plants with the promise that they would sell their crops exclusively to us.

Working through Lorenzo and our greenhouse grower Kathi, Marlin found additional growers around the state, and we ended up with our original field in Las Cruces, four superhot microfarms in Albuquerque, one in Hatch, and one in Florida. The most significant breakthrough was a business relationship with Jimmy Lytle in Hatch, a living legend in the New Mexico chile pepper industry for developing the 'Big Jim' variety of New Mexican chile, named after his father. His one thousand plants were so productive that he suggested to Marlin that they should utilize his equipment to dehydrate the superhot pods, adding a new dimension to value-added superhot products. Lytle is planning to increase his superhot plantings to five acres in 2015.

In early August 2014, Marlin, Gillie, and I visited all four South Valley, Albuquerque microfarms and were very impressed with the heavy fruiting of green pods. I started calculating the number of harvestable plants in all these fields because that's a better first-indicator of potential profit than projected dollars.

In 2013, we had only 3,100 harvestable plants in two microfarms. In 2014, at this writing, we had 8,225 harvestable plants in seven microfarms, so we nearly tripled production in one year. Based on all the fields that have produced better than ours in Las Cruces, the plan now is to become processors and producers of wholesale superhot products like the forms dried, mash, and frozen.

What I've learned from this microfarm project is that you've got to take the long view. Experimental microfarms like this one take time because the learning process evolves every year. I know now to avoid selling superhot chiles as produce and focus on turning that produce into more valuable and storable commodities. And next year, I will be in charge of all the growers in Albuquerque, and I'm planning on tripling production.

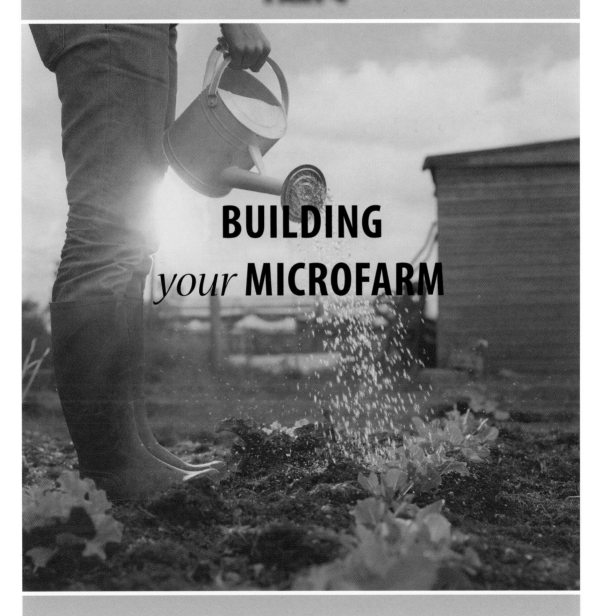

PART 4

BUILDING
your MICROFARM

In this section, I'm going to give you aspiring microfarmers a step-by-step approach to building your own microfarm, starting with tools needed for the farm, the constructions of a cold frame, hoop house and greenhouse, building raised beds, and other ways to increase crop yields.

Tools You Didn't Know You'd Need

From garden clippers to a rake to a shovel, I'm not going to detail all the ordinary tools a microfarmer will need to grow crops, because, as you come to realize what you need, you'll buy it or borrow it and that will be that. Rather, I'm going to focus on the specialized tools that will assist you more than you ever realized in achieving your farming goals.

Electric Cultivator. If you follow my microfarm plan with the greenhouse and raised beds described below, you won't need to buy, rent, or borrow an $800 gasoline-powered rototiller because you won't be breaking new ground, so to speak. In other words, you won't need the power of those devices because you will be working with a far more cooperative soil mix in a raised bed than in your backyard dirt. Since my nephew Max has a rototiller, I've never bought a cultivator, but if I had to, I'd get an electric one like the GreenWorks Electric Cultivator by Global Industrial that, as of this writing, sells for $156.95. Since you'll be mixing or cultivating, not digging or rototilling, a lightweight electric one at a low price will work fine, without the bother of gasoline.

Staple Gun. You will need it to attach gardening fabric to the raised beds for weed prevention, and to affix plant identification labels to the beds, and for some greenhouse tasks. You won't need a powerhouse that requires great strength to use like the Arrow W-T-50 that weighs in at two pounds. Instead buy an Arrow SW-JT-21 that weighs half as much, is easy to squeeze, and costs about $15.00.

Caulking Gun. All fiberglass or polycarbonate greenhouse roofs leak at some time in their existence, and you will need a standard caulking gun to repair those leaks, and keep the rain out and the heat in during the winter. These cost around $10.00.

Hand Truck. You've only got two arms and one back, so make moving things easier for yourself by using a hand truck, sometimes called a dolly. Do not get a cheap flimsy one for moving large pots, bags of steer manure, and other heavy things. Get one with real, pneumatic tires that converts from vertical to horizontal moving like the Milwaukee Hand Truck No. 40611, with a convertible 600-pound capacity, currently selling for $113.

Wheelbarrow or Garden Cart. You're going to need one or the other of these to move or mix soil and move pots and bags of manure around. I recently did an online search to replace my garden cart with the cracked bottom, and I found a hybrid, a wheelbarrow with two tires on the front end for stability and a deep tray that would hold six cubic feet of material. It's a True Temper Poly Wheelbarrow with Dual Wheels and it costs about $90. That's the one I'll buy.

In addition to all these tools, you should learn about the various structures you may need to increase the efficiency and production of your microfarm.

The Microfarm Cold Frame

Depending on what you grow and how you grow it, you may or may not need a cold frame or two in your microfarm. Think of a cold frame as a miniature, unheated greenhouse that shares a wall with your residence or your greenhouse. Typically, bedding plants were started in the greenhouse but before putting them in the garden soil, the plants were placed in the cold frame to harden-off—that is, adapt to a colder environment. They are not designed as plant growing structures, but you could start seeds in one.

Back in the day, cold frames usually consisted of a wooden or block framework about two and a half feet high and five or six feet long that was topped with old windows. They always faced the south in order to capture a maximum amount of sunlight. These days you can purchase pre-made cold frames in a variety of shapes and sizes using either greenhouse film or polycarbonate for the roof.

I don't need a cold frame for my microfarm, because I'm not concerned about the plants adjusting to cold temperatures. I worry about the plants adjusting to the high winds of spring and the strong ultraviolet rays at one mile above sea level. So I harden-off my plants by placing them in semi-shade for a few days and then gradually moving them into the sun. At night, they're back in the greenhouse with the temperature set low.

If you don't intend to keep plants alive over the winter, a cold frame could replace a greenhouse for spring germination and then some amount of hardening-off. Growers Supply sells a polycarbonate rectangular cold frame that's about 7.5 feet long and 4 feet deep with an adjustable slanting roof that's 23 inches tall in the back and 17 inches tall in the front. It costs about $600, which is about one-eighth the total cost of a greenhouse. It is much smaller and less versatile than a greenhouse, but it may serve your purposes for less of an investment.

The Microfarm Hoop House

Microfarmers should have a hoop house, a greenhouse, or both. The hoop house, also called a poly-tunnel, is the more primitive of the two, lacking a heater and a ventilation system—it is heated by the sun and ventilated by the wind. A hoop house consists of a series of large hoops that are made of metal, PVC pipe, or even wood, covered with a layer of heavy greenhouse plastic. The plastic is stretched tight and fastened to baseboards with strips of wood, metal, or staples.

You can build one for a few hundred dollars or a few thousand dollars, depending on its size.

Hoop houses are primarily used to increase crop yields by extending the season from four to six weeks in the spring and fall. By adding heavy row covers at night, and maybe a small electric heater, you can grow cold-hardy varieties of lettuce and other greens or root crops like carrots and you can keep growing right through the winter. They can be as low to the ground as three feet or high enough for someone six feet tall to work in comfortably. One microfarmer featured in *Mother Earth News* was earning $2,500 a year from one hoop house 14 feet wide and 96 feet long, so if you wanted to be a hoop house microfarmer, you could fit ten of those easily on an acre of land.

Hoop houses can also be used during the summer—even to keep growing lettuce, spinach, other greens, or microgreens. To do this, the hoop house is transformed into a shade house by replacing the plastic with a fifty percent shade cloth and adding mini-sprinklers to keep the lettuce moist and cool.

A gardener's cold frame.
Photo by Stock Solutions.

Microfarmers can design and build their own by following various instructions after searching for "how to build a hoop house" online, or they can buy a kit. Hoophouse Greenhouse Kits (Hoophouse.com) has a 48-foot hoop house that's 10 feet wide and 7 feet tall. It comes with all parts, fasteners, and the plastic film. All you have to buy is some plywood and framing lumber. The cost is about a thousand dollars for one this size.

Some farmers build portable hoop houses by building them in 16-foot sections that can be moved by two people to cover new beds they are starting. Three of these would make a 48-foot hoop house like the one mentioned above. Microfarmers will have to price homemade versus kits, and then compare kit prices in order to find the one that best fits their needs.

The Microfarm Greenhouse

I have described my microfarm greenhouse in Part 3, but that's not the only type of greenhouse you can use. I have checked the specs of quite a few greenhouse systems and the ones I like best are those from Solar Star, sold by Growers Supply (GrowersSupply.com). They use greenhouse film rather than polycarbonate for the roof, but the specs say the life of the film is four years, which is good for polyethylene. The greenhouse ends are polycarbonate. Each greenhouse kit comes with a natural gas or propane heater, one door kit, an exhaust fan with shutters, a circulation fan, the greenhouse film, and a waterproof thermostat. The smallest kit builds a greenhouse that's 12 feet wide, 8 feet tall, and 16 feet long and it sells for $3,055.

You would have to build the floor or have a contractor do it. A drain in the middle of the floor is recommended, and you can pour a concrete slab, or lay down patio stones, or even build a grid out of lumber, fill it with gravel, and install the greenhouse on top of it. I do not recommend just placing the greenhouse on grass or soil—it must have good drainage. Of course, the cost of building the floor is extra, as are the benches you will need for the plants. The printed catalog of Growers Supply has eight pages devoted to greenhouse benches, and the rest of the 354-page catalog has everything a microfarmer would ever need.

The basic uses of the greenhouse in

A microfarmer inspects his hoop house.
Photo by Bob Zemuda.

microfarming are:

—Wintering over potted plants, like the chile peppers I mentioned in Part 3.

—Germinating seeds for bedding plants in the spring.

—Growing herbs and greens during the winter.

—Using it as a solar food dehydrator in the summer.

Only you can decide which of these three structures—or which combination of them—will work best in your microfarm. But no matter what you're using to germinate and grow bedding plants, the summer home for those plants should be raised beds.

Building Raised Beds

I believe that for a microfarm, the most efficient and cost-effective way to grow most crops is not directly in the ground, but rather on top of the ground in carefully prepared beds that allow for rapid root growth and proper drainage, which are critical for maximum crop yields. Here are some of the advantages of using raised beds rather than direct, in-ground planting:

—You can better control the growing medium. I use a mixture of what the big box home stores call bagged top soil (a combination of forest wood products, compost, sandy loam, and gypsum), steer manure, and perlite. I don't have to worry

Raised beds are the most efficient and cost-effective way to go.
Photo by Srl.

about soil compaction because I'm not using any yard soil, which has a lot of clay in it, and the plants' roots expand very quickly.

— The plants in raised beds can be spaced closer together, increasing the microfarm's productivity per square foot planted.

— By laying down drip hoses and then covering the beds with garden cloth before you plant, then covering the garden cloth with mulch after planting, you will have reduced or completely eliminated weeds from the beds.

— The improved drainage and mulch will reduce water costs.

— The raised beds offer relief from unnecessary bending and eases planting, tending, and harvesting.

The first two beds I built were made out of two-by-sixes hammered together to form four by eight feet beds that were six inches deep. These worked fine as long as the ground was rototilled first and loosened up before placing the raised bed wooden frame on top of it. Commercial soil and steer manure were added to fill up the bed. But the new bed I built for microfarming in 2013 was even better.

This time I used railroad ties, which required no nailing. They weren't going anywhere and because they were treated, they would last a lifetime, unlike the two-by-sixes. It took eight ties stacked on top of each other in a square, and the resulting raised bed was a foot high and eight and a half feet square, making a growing area that totaled about 72 square feet and cost, so far, about $90. But then I had to fill about a thousand cubic feet of space with a growing medium.

My yardman, Clay Garner, whose crew does the spring yard cleanup here, provided a pickup load of top soil for $20, and then I spent about a hundred more for bagged top soil and double

that in steer manure from a big box home store, which was the only fertilizer I used. So this raised bed cost a little over $350, but after it was thoroughly rototilled (I could have just cultivated it), it produced tomato plants more than six feet tall and half that wide, loaded with large fruits. In fact, it produced three times the yield of the older raised beds, which were a total of 96 square feet, but only half as deep.

But since I built those beds, there have been advances in raised bed technology which I will adopt for my next raised bed. Instead of two-by-sixes or railroad ties, I'm going to use the PolyMax® Raised Bed Kits. The panels for beds are made from twenty percent wood fiber and plastic that's light and maintenance-free, so they won't rot, crack, or split like wood does. A typical PolyMax® bed that's four-by-eight-feet with 11-inch wide panels costs about $270, but it will be much easier to assemble—or even move—than the two previous beds.

Expanding the Microfarm

Let's just say that sometime in the future you have maxed out your land for microfarming and you want to expand your operation without necessarily buying more land. One way is by sharefarming. Sharefarming agreements are now fairly common, and the microfarmer can select the land and negotiate one of three different scenarios.

— Microfarmers can rent plots of land from the owner for a certain sum and keep the whole crop.

— Microfarmers work on the land and earn a fixed wage from the landowner and keep some of the crop.

— No money changes hands but the microfarmer and landowner each keep a share of the crop, with the larger percentage going to the farmer. A more permanent solution is available as well.

The Center for Rural Affairs in Lyons, Nebraska, operates a service called Land Link. According to their website, it is "an opportunity for beginning farmers and ranchers and established landowners to work together to secure their farming futures." Asset transferring usually follows one of the following options:
—Outright Sale: Owner of property sells it outright to the beginning farmer or rancher.
—Installment Sale: Owner sells asset to the beginner over time.
—Gradual Sale: Sale of single assets over a period of years. For example, sale of one piece of machinery each year, or sale of fixed number of cattle each year.
—Leasing: Lease is often combined with one of the preceding asset transfer tools.
—Gift: A person can gift up to $12,000 each year to another person without tax consequences.
—Trusts or Entities: A trust may be used to accomplish the transfer of assets over time to a beginner.

The business structures to accomplish this range from partnerships to various types of corporations. The website (cfra.org/landlink) has a number of success stories using all the transfer options mentioned, and one of these scenarios might fit your needs for expansion. Other organizations doing similar work include:

National Farmer and Rancher Linking Programs

These programs are designed to transition farm and ranch land from one generation to the next.

International Farm Transition Network Listings: These are linking programs across the United States. The goal of the network is to support programs that foster the next generation of farmers and ranchers. It develops programs that link retirement and farm exit strategies with farm entry strategies. Programs representing at least twenty states have established Farm Link programs to "link" beginning and retiring farmers. (FarmTransition.org)

Rodale Institute's New Farm Classifieds: These classified ads frequently list linkage opportunities. According to their website, "you will be asked to create an account and login, meaning you control just how public or private your information is. From there you can post a classified ad, start a discussion thread or chat with the folks already talking on their Facebook page." (RodaleInstitute.org/farm/farmers-connect/)

MOSES' Land Link-Up: These are more classified ads frequently listing linkage opportunities. According to their website, "MOSES offers this free online service in an effort to connect those looking for farmland with those looking to rent or sell farmland." (MosesOrganic.org/farming/land-link-up/)

100 Beef Cow Ownership Advantage Program: According to their website, "this program has been created to provide a forum where students, parents, employers, and agencies can come together to create successful business plans and ranch transfer programs. For the past two decades, state and federal agencies, legislatures, and commodity groups have worked hard to develop programs that encourage the transfer of agricultural enterprises to the next generation." (Ncta.Unl.edu/100cowprogram)

Gardener Linking Programs: These programs connect people with land to people who want to have a large garden or a microfarm.

Urban Land Army's Land Link (national): "Land Link is an Urban Land Army project with a nice idea: they connect people who have land with people who want to garden." (Urbanlandarmy.com)

Urban Gardenshare (Seattle and seven other cities): This program matches "homeowners (with garden space) to gardeners (with experience) and is the perfect solution for cultivating both food production and community." (UrbanGardenShare.org)

But, before you even think about expansion, you should learn how to make money with your microfarm, and that means selling what you are growing.

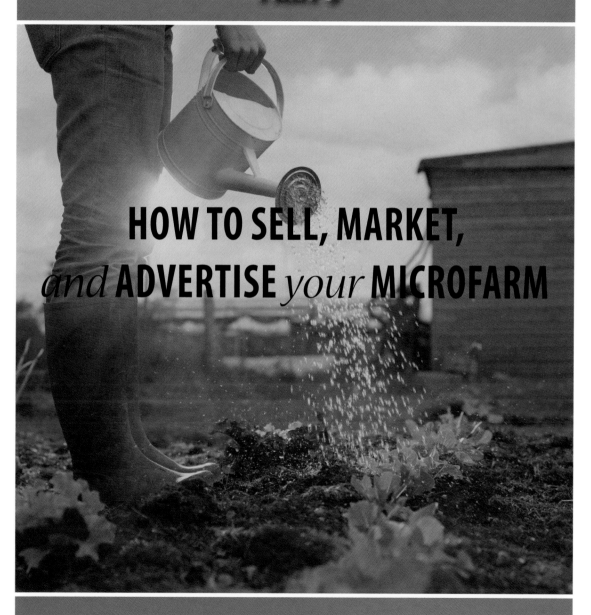

PART 5

HOW TO SELL, MARKET, *and* **ADVERTISE** *your* **MICROFARM**

Marketing and sales are just as important as a good harvest in the microfarming business. If you are reticent about sales and learning how to sell, do not start a microfarm. This aspect of microfarming is of crucial importance and cannot be ignored.

How I Learned How to Sell

When I was in college studying literature and learning how to write, I never imagined that I would turn out to be a pretty damned good sales person. Here's how it happened. While in college, then graduate school, then teaching college English for freshmen and sophomores, I also had part-time jobs in the radio business. I was an on-air personality—okay, I was a DJ, but I didn't like it all that much because of the constraints placed on all the announcers: follow the format, don't talk too much, and move the show along. Not very creative. I preferred working in the production departments of these stations, producing radio commercials.

By writing commercials, I learned a lot about radio advertising because I had to interact with the sales people, finding out what their clients wanted. And I got to suggest themes for the commercials, or contests, or promotions. But I wasn't planning on working in radio for my main career because I was teaching college. I was in the world of academia and almost got seduced into believing that I would stay in the university system, get my Ph.D., and write literary criticism. Wrong. As it turned out, radio—and later media and advertising in general—was more fun and, in many ways, more creative.

When my three-year teaching contract expired, I was seriously thinking of applying for a full-time job at the radio station. Then I met my neighbor across the street, Don. He, too, was in radio, but in a totally different way. He sold radio promotion services to stations in small towns in the Deep South, like Mississippi. He offered me a deal: go down to Mississippi to small towns and sell participation in the promotions to local businesses by making cold calls door to door.

"But I know nothing about door-to-door sales," I protested.

"Not a problem," Don said. "I'll teach you. I learned from the best. You could make five hundred dollars a week." That was significant money in 1971. I was twenty-five years old and I had nothing to lose.

"I'll go for the summer," I told him. He had closed me.

He spent the rest of his vacation giving me a hard-core sales lesson, and it was fascinating. He was into sales like proselytizers are into religion. He wrote out his goals each morning and he often used legendary pitchman and motivational speaker Zig Ziglar's trademark slogan, "See you at the top!" Don pasted his big goals on his bathroom mirror. A yacht. A Bentley. A treasure chest filled with gold coins. He was and still is the best salesman I ever met. Not the most honest, mind you—merely the best.

My training involved learning the "nest principle" of selling radio promotions, which meant that you pitched all the Sunoco dealers in the county an exclusive gas station deal. Then, he showed me how to approach the shops and garage owners when selling them Radio Bingo, how to do an effective flip-card presentation, how to counter objections, the ten basic closes, and how and when to use them. The minor-decision close, the assumptive close, and even the last ditch piss-on-their-foot close. Don told me if the owner throws you out of his place but doesn't spit on you, it's a weak maybe. Then how to collect the money, and be sure to go over all the details of Radio Bingo with the customer, then do it again.

Day after day we went through this. I had to memorize the entire flip-card presentation that we would give a customer. Don made me keep rehearsing it, and then played the role of the customer and made objection after objection to see if I could overcome them. I felt like I was getting an M.A. in sales. Ironically, I would later become sales manager of a radio station.

I could go on for fifty pages about my Radio Bingo sales adventures in Mississippi, Tennessee, and West Virginia, but I won't. Suffice it to say that it was wild and crazy, with drugs, sex, and rock 'n roll of youth, along with the sobering twenty-five sales calls each day for each of us, on our feet, door-to-door in places like War, West Virginia, and Itta Bena, Mississippi (I'm not making these up). I made excellent money, all in cash, and participated in the closest thing to a con scheme I have ever experienced. But the sales lessons and hands-on experience Don hammered into me have stayed with me since. I use several of his tricks every day of my life, and I'll always remember his expression for the hard work ahead, "Ain't no easy run, son."

Below, I've outlined a step-by-step sales manual for microfarmers.

The Elements of a Sale

It doesn't matter whether you're selling radio promotions or organic produce—the essential elements of a sale are basically the same. You have to make minor adjustments along the way, but the point I'm trying to make is to formulate a plan and follow it. Base your plan on the steps below, and at least you will have a direction to go and an organized approach. If it's in your mind that "I don't want to learn any of this sales stuff, I just want to be in my field taking care of my crops," then you better find someone who *does* want to learn this sales stuff, because it has to be done. It doesn't matter who takes on the sales work in your family or farm business, but someone has to be the leader in bringing the money in to keep the operation going.

Know Your Products

This seems rather obvious but you might be surprised at how slapdash some people are about sales. It's the "let's just throw everything in a box and take it to the farmers' market and peddle it" approach, and you have to avoid that. Again, make a plan. Write down all your products from the baby beets to the pickled asparagus (or whatever) that are your value-added products. Then write out a description of each product. What variety of beets are they? What kind of dishes can you make out of them? Roasted beets

Your customers expect you to be the expert about what you're selling. Photo by Dave DeWitt.

with balsamic vinegar dusted with chile powder? Why not provide a recipe that the customer can take with her along with those beets? That's a value-added sales method.

How did you make those pickled asparagus spears that you're trying to sell? What can they be used for? Write it down so you'll remember it if a customer asks. You must be a master of details about the foods you're selling. You're the farmer, after all, the expert. The customers will expect you to know all these things and they will respect you when you give them good information. And that beet recipe you're giving

Simple chalkboards make effective signage and can be easily changed. Photo by Caroline Culler.

them? Did you handwrite it on a scrap of paper and photocopy it, or did you type it out on your computer, proof it for errors, and put your farm logo at the top and contact information at the bottom? You must be professional about every contact you have with the customer. You want happy customers because they will be repeat customers.

Find Your Specific Market and Customers

This seems totally obvious, too. But the farmers who don't do this kind of research and just depend on traffic going by their space at the growers' market are like the two vultures on telephone poles just waiting around for some animal to die. Finally, one of the vultures turns to the other one and says, "To hell with all this waiting—let's go kill something!" You don't have to be that extreme, but why depend on the fickle retail customers who are trying to get the

cheapest prices on those beets at the market? Why don't you try to sell them all in one shot to chefs at restaurants? You could easily do that through an email newsletter that goes out the day before the market opens. "I've got perfect, delicious baby beets at the downtown growers' market tomorrow," you write to these selected chefs. "Better get there early before they're all gone." Some chefs are bound to show up, but remember that most of them will check out your produce first, and then come back at the close of the market and try to buy what you haven't sold for half price. Better make sure that doesn't happen.

Of course, you won't just have beets at that market—I'm only using that as an example. But if you're growing heirloom tomatoes, you will have a lot of competition because every grower usually has some at his or her stall at the market. One growers' market I know of fixed the prices that farmers were allowed to sell the tomatoes for. In 2013 it was $4.00 per tomato! This infuriated my farmer friend Lorenzo so much that he refused to work that market, and instead held his own market during the summer season every Saturday morning at his farm. He sent his customers an email or a text on Friday telling them that he had better produce at better prices than the growers' market. Meanwhile, I was sun-drying my tomatoes and then lightly smoking them in the smoker in order to make a great, unusual value-added product that was much more valuable than a single ripe tomato, and one that would have a much longer shelf life. When there are no more ripe tomatoes at that market at season's end, my sun-dried ones would be ready to go—if I had gone in that direction. But I prefer to sell to chefs.

Once you have focused in on the specific markets and customers you want to sell to, the next step is to make a sales plan, and the first step in doing that is to do a budget. A boring task? Only if you make it that way. You must spend money to make sales—it's a fact of business. So why not figure out how much you can afford to spend to make these sales happen?

Determine Your Sales Budget and Prepare Sales Materials

Small business owners often think that they cannot afford to advertise their business. I believe that you can't afford *not* to advertise. Handing out flyers? Collecting email addresses? It's all advertising. You have to master these skills or pay someone to do it, but it has to happen to secure your success. And remember, you're in it for the long haul, and advertising is cumulative and progressive. If you are persistent, success will follow.

Need signage for your space at the market? That's going to cost, so figure out the signs you will need, get an estimate from sign makers, then decide which to use and put that figure in your budget. With each retail sale you make, you want to put a flyer in the bag with their beets, so add printing expenses to that budget. And the cost of the bags. Eventually you'll want to have your own shopping bags to give to really good customers and sell to the others. Not plastic, but cloth with your logo on them. In the meantime, substitute paper bags that you collect at the supermarkets and retail stores where you shop. When asked by the clerk, plastic or paper, you'll know what to say.

Office supplies, business cards, and even some appropriate clothing for working the market should go on that budget. A wardrobe for working the market, you ask? Are you crazy?

How about jeans and a t-shirt? Okay, but that t-shirt should have your farm logo on it. You have to at least look organized and professional. More on this later.

Here's a modest start-up marketing plan for a microfarm. All the costs are approximate for this sample.

Logo Design: $400. The right name for your microfarm is the first step in building your brand. The next is establishing a "look" for your company with some sort of logo that you will use in all signs, correspondence, stationery, invoices, advertising, and publicity. This is called marketing consistency. Forget about hiring your cousin's daughter to create your logo because she's such a good painter. Those are two completely different skill sets, and you don't need a fine artist, you need a commercial or graphic artist, one who's an advertising professional. Keep the logo simple because it's not a picture, it's a symbolic representation of what your agricultural enterprise is. And you shouldn't over-think it, because some logos will be obvious, depending on the name of your microfarm. A good commercial artist will have no trouble whatsoever showing you four different roughs of a logo for Green Tractor Farm or Twin Crows Farm.

The artist should deliver the logo in at least two formats: .JPG for the simple stuff and .EPS for more complicated projects. The great thing about .EPS is that it's a vector format, meaning that it can be re-sized without affecting image quality.

Business Cards: $50. Once you have a logo, cards are cheap, from either your local print shop or several online vendors.

T-shirts: $66. Use CafePress.com and you can

put your logo on a shirt for $22. You should get three to start.

Email Newsletter: $168. iContact.com charges you $14 a month for up to 500 subscribers. This will be a year's worth. You can find a template with a garden design and modify it for your own use by adding your logo to it. There are many companies that provide such services, and I tried a lot of them before settling on iContact.com. If you only have a few subscribers, often the service is free until you exceed a certain number, then you pay by number of subscribers. There are templates available so you can customize your newsletter, adding your logo and various photos. Send your newsletter regularly, like bimonthly or weekly to alert your customers as to what foods you currently have available, or any specials, or to promote a line of products. The newsletter interface is easy to use, and doesn't require any specialized knowledge like coding.

Website: $500. You will need to register a domain and pay an internet service provider to host it. You can build your own website by using WordPress.com, and there is no charge for this. The estimated cost here includes registry and hosting plus paying a designer to make it look as nice as possible. A blog format would work in this situation to encourage customer interaction and create dialogs that entertain your readers. Through your blog or site, you can offer specials, conduct surveys, take crop requests, and encourage readers to forward your newsletter to other likeminded people who can then sign up to receive it. So far, in just a couple of years, 1,150 new subscribers have signed up for my weekly newsletter through the ad on my website's home page.

Banner Signage: $100. This will get you a nice-sized vinyl banner with grommets, perfect for hanging in a booth or behind a table. Sign makers have a saying, "No sign is a sign of no business," and if you extend that concept you will soon grasp the fact that advertising is not just a television campaign or a newspaper ad, it happens every single time you engage with the public—your potential customers. If you work farmers' markets on weekends, you'll need a nice banner to hang with your company name and logo on it.

The challenge is to make your produce stand out at market.
Photo by Britt Reints.

At a huge market like this one in downtown Austin, Texas, you'll need every trick in the book to make your booth memorable to customers. Photo by Lars Plougmann.

Flyers: $150. Or a tenth of that if you have a photocopier. This should last an entire year.

The total cost for your start-up plan is $1,452. Okay, you have a budget, so now implement it. All of your sales material, from business cards to flyers, from signage to recipe sheets should have your logo on them and look professional. Advertising agents call this a unified campaign—you want to send the same message in all media with the same, professional look. And remember, you will only have to spend most of this money once.

Social media. Social media has a place in advertising your microfarm if you don't overdo it. Do I like Facebook? Not particularly. Do I use Facebook as an advertising medium, paid or not? Yes. Twitter? Yawn, but I use it regularly for announcements of my latest newsletter, to announce deadlines, and generally to connect with customers and fans. But do I read other people's tweets? No. How about YouTube? I have presence there, but not a large one, and frankly, it hasn't generated much business for me that I can quantify. How about all the other ones, like Google+, Pinterest, StumbleUpon, Reddit, Newsvine, LinkedIn, and Tumblr? I've never used any of them and probably won't. I'm already using three social media sites, plus my own website, and an email newsletter. That's five marketing systems to manage, and enough is enough. You can get bogged down in social media by too much non-business participation, and you should remember that social media is in a constant state of flux, with one site suddenly popular until the next one comes along and beats it.

Other forms of advertising. From flyers on telephone poles to zip-targeted mailings to outdoor billboards to banner ads on other websites and blogs, there are a lot of ways to spend—and waste—your money. Hold these in check for at least the first year of your microfarm because most are out of your budget completely. Focus on the basics above that lead to more sales immediately and don't worry about advertising that the salespeople tell you will build your brand. Reply that you're already building it, from the ground up, and see if they get the pun.

Everyone's a salesperson. But most people don't know that, or don't believe that, or can't imagine that they can play that role. As a kid, did you ever convince your parents to let you stay up later than normal to watch some special TV show? Then you made a sale. Did you ever ask someone for a date and they agreed? You made a sale, and even though it cost you money, you achieved something you wanted. Who knew that my wife, Mary Jane, whose only real career had been teaching high school English classes, would turn into one of the best phone salespersons I have ever met? With her, it's just the gift of gab.

The sales process has been around for millennia and it's very simple. You prospect for leads. You qualify those leads. You pitch those leads a product or service. You close the sale. You collect the money. You start the process all over again. Whether you're selling a tomato at the farmers' market, or selling a booth in a trade show, or selling a car on a lot, it's the same process.

In a microfarm situation, you prospect through your website, the newsletter, and a professional-looking booth at a market or show. You collect email addresses, you hand out business cards and/or flyers, you charm the potential customers, you ask them questions or counter objections, you give them a small deal to get them to buy more. This is qualifying the prospects.

"I'll come back later," a woman says.

"I probably won't be here," you reply. "I usually sell out early. If you spend twenty dollars, I'll give you this free shopping bag." With your company logo on it, of course.

That's not so hard, is it?

The rest of the sales process. So far, all the above are just the basics and designed for selling your farmed goods on the most basic levels—fresh from the farm with maybe a few simple, value-added products like, say, homemade sundried tomatoes or bagged mixed salad greens. If you decide to create real value-added products, then your advertising will become a lot more sophisticated.

Most people who know about gardening or farming know their crops, and don't mind talking to people can become good salespeople. Yes, it takes practice, just like anything else. But as you gain sales experience, you'll not only become a better salesperson, you'll be making money along the way.

Start Prospecting

The entire sales process comes down to finding people who want to buy what you have to sell, and to do that you must winnow down a large group of potential customers to a much smaller group. You also have to manage the customers you already have. I have found that the easiest way to do both is to use mass emails on a regular basis. Most vendors who supply these services have sophisticated methods of maintaining lists and mailing professional-looking newsletters to these lists.

There are built-in safeguards with such a process; for example, the programs used will not allow duplicate emails to be sent to contacts. So you could send your email to two different lists without worrying that someone will get the same email more than once. Since most of the companies providing these services require that people give you their permission before you email them, the best way to start is to have an email newsletter signup sheet wherever you display your products in public. If someone writes their name and email on the signup sheet, they have given you permission to email them. If they don't like your emails they can opt out of the list automatically—you don't have to take any action at all. This process allows some slippage—in other words, if you prospect for leads that have not given permission, you can slip a few of these emails into your list without much worry because these people can opt out with a single click. And, for the most part, existing customers are fair game for these lists because you've dealt with them before.

To encourage people to give you their email addresses, you can have a drawing for, say, $25 worth of your produce or products, with the winner announced each week in your newsletter.

That's the way we collect email addresses through the Fiery Foods & Barbecue Show we produce, and it works quite well.

Your email newsletters to prospects or customers should be professional-looking, short, and to the point. Stick to business—these people couldn't care less about your personal beliefs, so keep philosophy, religion, politics, and sports out of them. A simple email during the growing season could inform customers of where you will be selling your beets or rutabagas and what specials you have. That's all. No need to tell them about your new niece or the fact your daughter is getting married—they don't know these people and don't care. This is not Facebook. If you bore them, they will opt out—guaranteed.

Find out what the policies of these email companies are. I was shocked to find out that some of them do not allow you to mail to companies that have supposedly anonymous email addresses like info@companyA.com, or management@companyB.com. They require names like ben@companyA.com. But this policy will be too limiting for you because so many people have no imagination and just go with an anonymous approach. So don't use companies that have this policy, which has never made any sense to me.

Manage the Leads

If you are selling retail to the public *and* wholesale to chefs, caterers, and manufacturers, it makes sense to have a list for each one. You can break them down into subcategories like Wholesale-Chefs, if you need to. By having a large number of specific lists, you can better target the leads you'd like to reach with a certain email.

Make sure you always include one photo with your email. Maybe it's your daughter holding up a perfect beet, or your carrots with a rabbit next to them and the headline, Buy These Before They're All Gone. The more entertaining you are, the more often your email will be opened, and the better your response rate. You can easily track the percentage of people who open your emails, but their effectiveness can only be measured by increased sales over a significant period of time. And of course, your emails will only be part of your sales effort. But it's much more efficient than trying to call them on the phone, and a lot less expensive than snail mail.

For your wholesale customers, this is a lot like fishing. You've cast the bait out there, and you will get some responses. Usually it would be one of your customers or would-be customers who replies with some line like, "I'd like to take a look at the quality of your beets. Could you drop some by?" To which you would reply, "What's a good time for you, Chef Roberts?"

Make the Calls and Pitches

When you make sales calls, be sure your appearance is nice. I don't mean a coat and tie, but no muddy jeans and ripped t-shirts, either. It goes without saying to be prompt, assuming you have made an appointment, and when you get to meet the chef or other wholesale buyer, don't take up a lot of his or her time. This is a very simple pitch, so unless they ask, don't start telling the story of how you became a microfarmer or why your produce is superior to that of your competition.

Remember that every buyer is looking for a deal, and you will probably be asked to lower your prices several times on each call. When a

potential buyer does that, they are making an objection that must be overcome, and there are several ways to do that. Here's how that scenario might play out.

"It's the same price that Chef Bryan is paying over at The Pink Balloon," you tell the prospect.

"But it's more than my budget."

"You actually have a beet budget?" you ask.

"Let's just say it's more than I'm willing to pay."

"The only way I can lower the price is if you buy more beets from me—after all, they keep well."

"Let me think about it." This is a maybe, and you don't want maybes because they're a waste of time. What does this prospect want—that you should bug him about beets every day?

"What's to think about? Buy twice the weight I quoted you and I'll knock ten percent off the total price."

If your original price was outrageous, the prospect would have immediately said something like, "You want me to pay the retail price?" But in this situation the chef is either being a cheapskate, really watching his money, or just doing it to see if he can beat you, so to speak. But you have made him a fair counter-offer, so if he needs the beets he'll probably buy them. If he still refuses and you lower the price more, you're playing the chef's game. Here's how it could go from this point.

The chef says no. You offer your hand and say, "Sorry we couldn't work this out; nice to meet you." Or "nice seeing you" if you've met the person before.

The chef says yes. You say: "Great! I have them in the cooler in my Jeep. Cash, check, or card?" (See below about taking the money.)

By countering the objection, you made the sale, so that was a close, too. But there are many more closes.

Close the Sale

Say you're making calls on chefs to sell them beets for their restaurants, and one of them is balking at making the buy but won't give you a reason, like money. Obviously you need a close that will counter any objection he has. But if you can't figure out what the guy or gal's objection is, what close do you use? I'll get back to this in a moment. My mentor in show production, the late, great Frank Crosby, had one of the most unique closes I've ever witnessed. I call it the hang-around-and-tell-jokes-until-the-customer-buys-or-throws-you-out close. And being a former vaudeville comedian, Frank had tons of corny jokes. Frank was a recycled Henny Youngman, but very funny.

I accompanied him to a yard maintenance company that sold lawnmowers and such. Frank pitched the owner, a regular customer, for twenty minutes or so, but the guy wouldn't budge and wouldn't make a decision, even when Frank tried the repeat customer discount close: "Last year's exhibitors get a seven percent discount." No response, so Frank went into joke mode and made the guy laugh a couple of times. Finally, after ten minutes of jokes, the owner shook his head, looked at his watch and said, "Frank, if I sign this damn contract, will you get the hell out of my office so I can get some work done?"

Frank smiled. "Sure, if you'll sign a check for the deposit, too."

Not too many salespeople can pull off that close and get a sale, but here are some basic closes you can try.

Assumptive Close. If the chef, distributor, or caterer is a regular customer and you know they like your rutabagas, why not drop off a bag of them with an invoice attached? If they balk: "I wasn't going to offer creamed rutabagas on the menu this week," then try the:

Exclusivity Close. "Well, Chef Shirley over at Wangdoodles wanted these, but you're my best customer so I figured I should give you first selection." This is also called Ego-Appeal Close, and it doesn't work with chefs who have any sales experience.

Minor Decision Close. "Do you want the white corn, the yellow corn, or a mix?" is a good example of this because it's two closes in one. You've assumed the chef's going to buy, so all that's left is his or her trifling decision about which one to buy. You've switched the customer from the big decision to the small one.

Impending Event Close. You're selling at a growers' market. All produce eventually goes bad, so a basic version of this one for the microfarmer is some variation of the it's-all-going-to-rot-and-I'll-have-to-throw-it-out-if-you-don't-buy-it close. Or say, "I have to leave the market early today, so make a decision, chef." This gets the chef to say yay or nay, which is good either way—you have a fifty percent shot at getting the sale. A no is not bad, because it ends the sale and doesn't waste your time. If someone gives you a maybe and says they'll come back later, or asks you to come by the restaurant, say no and make her decide on the spot. Or joke, "And maybe I'll eat at your restaurant some time."

Lack of Supply Close. This is a variation of the Impending Event Close. Always tell the truth, so don't use this if it's not true. "It's late in the season and I'm almost out of beets. These may be the last I can supply you, and I know they're scarce around town." Try not to be too outlandish, like "I just read an entomologist's report that a cloud of turnip weevils is headed for the South Valley, so these may be the last beets of the year."

Piss-On-Their-Foot Close. Please don't take this one literally—it's a figure of speech. Save it for the last resort. You probably don't have a chance to make a sale, but you'll never see this person again in your life, so give it a try. Here's a real example of how it works. Years ago, my friend Jorge Midón was driving his truck from Albuquerque all the way down to some farm in Yucatán, picking up a load of luffa sponges, and driving them back here. Luffa sponges are gourds that are a common bath and beauty aid now, but were unknown to consumers in the mid '70s. We worked two state fairs to sell them all. The first one was the seventeen-day endurance test of the New Mexico State Fair, and curious customers would come up, look at the luffas, and say, "My, that's interesting. What are these luffa things?" That was a salesperson's dream opening to start a pitch, and we did very, very well at that fair. Then came the sheer torture of the twenty-three-day State Fair of Texas in Dallas where the usual comment from the men was, "What the hell is this crap?"

My usual response was to reply, "With a vulgar attitude like that, I'd never let the likes of you buy anything I was selling." Usually this would get the women giggling.

Then I would start my pitch in my best Southern accent. "You gals know about exfoliatin' your skin, right?" They would nod eagerly, curious now. Undoubtedly they read beauty magazines. "Well this is the latest natural beauty aid for doin' just that. Let me show you." I took one of the gal's hands and rubbed a moist, scented luffa over it, and the rest, as we say in the biz, was a done deal. The obnoxious guy bought the woman ten bucks worth of "that crap." Remember, when they reach for their wallets, the close has worked, it's over, and it's time to simply take their money. Another piece of advice: when presenting the close to the customer, think only about the goal of closing a sale, not the money you will make. That's too distracting and a later part of the sales plan, anyway. I made a huge number of sales that day using variations on that technique. At ten bucks a pop, it adds up.

Collect the Money

Why lose a sale because the customer has run out of cash? You want to have as much technology on your side as possible, and you can in this day and age. Accept credit and debit cards. You're thinking, *What a pain in the ass. I have to get a credit card terminal, have electrical service at my stand. It's just too much trouble.* Not anymore—all of that can be accomplished with an app and a small device you plug into your cell phone that you run the cards through. The money is immediately transferred into your checking account. There are several of these devices on the market, but the one I use and like is called the Square Card Reader from the website SquareUp.com.

Have a sign that shows the cards you take, and be sure to have a lot of small bills to make change with. If you're using a scale for the produce, round off the change to benefit the customer, if feasible. I don't know about you, but I hate pockets full of heavy change, so if the rutabagas they're buying come to $3.42, round it off to three bucks—they'll love it. But if it's something like $3.60, you could say, "I don't have any small change, but why don't you take another beet and make it an even four bucks?" Then again, if you don't mind change, use it—just be exact.

Do Post-Sale Maintenance

This is the customer service part of the sale. It's difficult to do this with all the people you sell to at a market, so just keep as many of them as you can in your email list and send them updates about what you'll have at the next market. But once you get to know your wholesale customers, you can get them to give you standing orders, like place an order for a certain poundage of beets every week. You can also have sales if you alert all your wholesale customers about it at the same time.

You will soon get to know these customers and discover their likes and dislikes. For example, my friend Matt Yohalem, who I supplied with tomato puree and culinary herbs during the 2013 season, likes unusually colored tomatoes and used my smoked sun-dried yellow tomatoes in a sauce on the side of a grilled fish dish, and thanked me on the daily menu. So next year I'm growing 'Golden Gem' (yellow), 'Chocolate Cherry' (dark purple), and 'Kellogg's Breakfast' (orange), specifically for sun-drying and smoking.

This brings up the question of custom-growing for chefs, which is a possible expansion of your current farm. As long as what a chef wants will fit into your growing system and it's not particularly difficult, I don't see many problems with it. You should have a signed agreement with the chef before you begin, however.

Selling at a Market or Show

Growers' markets and food events are great places to market your products because the people there are qualified prospects. But don't ruin your opportunity when you exhibit. Here's how *not* to work a stand at the growers' market or a booth in a show. Mary Jane and I produced the Albuquerque Home Show for a few years and once we sold a double booth to a housewares

To make the most of your time and investment, tand out, be friendly, and have fun at trade shows and other public events. Food seller: Anna Shawver of Apple Canyon Gourmet. Photo by Mark Masker.

retailer. I went by his setup and there were customers looking at his merchandise but he was in the back of his booth reading a book and watching a baseball game — multi-tasking with the wrong tasks. I casually mentioned to him that he would sell a lot more if he stood in the front of his booth and talked with his customers. He got irate.

"Look here, I paid good money for this booth and I'll do whatever I goddamn please in it. So leave me alone."

Well, excuuuuse me. After the show, he probably told all his business friends, "Don't do that Home Show next year — it doesn't work." Wrong. He didn't work the show, it's as simple as that.

When working a retail event, first make a sales goal, a figure in your mind of how much you want to gross that day. Then work like hell to accomplish it. Make it a game, a challenge to yourself and/or your staff. This process will format the mindset that you and your helpers, if any, are there to make money, and not just socialize with the public or friends that might come by.

Make sure that everyone working the stand or booth looks presentable. You might think of having some official-looking t-shirts or sport shirts made with your logo emblazoned on them, which would usually set you apart from the other vendors. Whoever is on point — that is, the main person greeting the public — should stand at all times and smile often. If the crowd is large, you might need two people on point to handle all the business. People don't like to wait to buy things — it's very much an impulse buy in many cases.

Every bit of produce you're selling should have an identification sign and a price — that will prevent having to repeat to everyone that the beets are five to the bunch and cost whatever.

Eli Burgione, profiled in Part 2, gives a head of garlic to anyone buying anything when he has the supply, and customers love that sort of thing. So if you have a bumper crop of something, consider doing it too. Unless business is slow, avoid long conversations with customers who are seeking growing advice, because this takes up time and prevents you from making sales to others. Here's how I would handle it.

"Wow, these beets could win the state fair," says the customer. "I sure wish I could grow beets this big. Mine are so puny. What do you think I'm doing wrong?" It would take at least twenty minutes to answer that, so you've got to get rid of him.

"I'm pretty busy here right now," you reply. "Take one of my cards and email me your growing technique and I'll get back to you with some ideas."

On your breaks from selling, get to know your fellow vendors. Connections are a good thing. Every vendor is more concerned with attracting customers than they are with worrying about you as a competitor. Be nice and friendly even if you hate their guts.

Agritourism

This term and microfarmer go hand in hand in a win-win situation. Mary Jane and I have visited four different *agriturismo* farms in Italy and stayed in three of them, and they were great fun. One was in the middle of a huge vineyard, and a lot of tasty wine and a nice cat helped us endure the rain. Another was Marco Del Freo and Maggie Wolf's farm outside of Parma that's perched at the top of a small mountain. They grow very hot chile peppers which are pressed fresh with olives to make a spicy first-pressing

Ca'd'Alfieri in Italy is a B&B and working farm—an excellent example of successful agritourism.
Photo by Harald Zoschke.

olive oil, and run a two-apartment B&B to generate even more income.

The best example I found of a multiple-use *agriturismo* farm was Ca'd'Alfieri ("Ca" is short for "Casa") outside of Bardi in northern Italy, about forty miles from Parma. Maurizio Bovi and Luisa Sgarbossa have renovated a 130-year-old house and turned it into a large B&B that looks over their microfarm. On the farm they raise all the produce necessary to feed their guests, as well as goats, chickens, and a variety of pig called 'Parmesan Black.' They also grow superhot chiles

for the European market, and have their own processing facility for value-added products like jams and jellies. Fresh fruit, produce, jams, jellies, and pickled products are offered for sale in the couples' retail store in Bardi, La Bottega di Ca' d'Alfieri. The store was designed to resemble a kitchen from the early 1900s, and it is decorated with rustic furniture and baskets made by local artisans, filled with products from their fields. There are no televisions or radios in the rooms, and cell phone service is sketchy at best. They have no swimming pool, no tennis courts, and no other amenities except great food and peace in the country.

Agritourism is getting big in the U.S. as well. North Carolina has an Agritourism Networking Association, and heavily promote the concept on their website. "Agritourism can be an exciting new enterprise for you," the site reads. "Hay rides, barnyard animals, corn mazes, pick-your-own fruits and vegetables, bird watching, farm roadside stands, fishing, hunting, camping, pumpkin patches, value-added products, flowers—let your imagination take you to your own field of dreams." The website agritourismworld.com has quite a bit of information on agritourism farms in the U.S. and around the globe.

Biodiversity and Sustainability for the Microfarmer

When I set thirty tomato or chile pepper plants in my microfarm, are all of those plants the same variety? No, of course not, because I'd like to avoid a small-scale replication of the Irish potato blight of 1846. Not only were all those potatoes the same variety, they were all the *same plant*! Because farmers grew tomatoes by cutting out the "eyes" and planting them, there was no chance for hybridization—all the potato plants were clones, so they all had the same amount of resistance to *Phytophthora infestans*, the fungus that killed them: none. This is what happens with monoculture crops and why biodiversity is so important no matter how large your growing operation is.

I'm not worried about Phytophthora because that disease is triggered by overwatering, which is nearly impossible in my extremely well-drained beds. I'm worried about curly top virus, transmitted by the beet leafhopper. Some varieties of nightshades like tomatoes and peppers have greater resistance to the virus than others, so I want to hedge my bet and vary the kinds I'm growing. One year, I planted numerous hybrids like 'Big Boy' and 'Early Girl,' and one heirloom variety, 'Black from Tula,' which had been prolific the previous year. We had a wet spring, which

meant an overabundance of London rocket, a weed in the mustard family that is a carrier for curly top. So when the leafhoppers hatched, they quickly attacked my plants. Most of the hybrids survived, but every single 'Black from Tula' plant, about twelve of them, sickened and had to be culled. If every tomato plant had been a 'Black from Tula,' it would have been a microdisaster.

So biodiversity in your microfarm is a good thing, and so is dollar-diversity, a term I've invented that refers to your sources of income and making sure that, as used to be said, all your eggs—or tomatoes—are not in one basket. This is why I've pushed value-added products so hard in this book and urged microfarmers to diversify. Just think back to the days when there was a Circle K or 7-Eleven on every other block. To survive, convenience store owners had to reinvent their business model, so they aligned with petroleum companies and became travel centers.

You've probably noticed that there are too many coffee shops, smoke shops, tattoo parlors, and fast food stores. They too will have to take a look at their dollar-diversity and reinvent their business models. Last year at the downtown growers' market, everyone was selling heirloom tomatoes. To level the playing field, the market

The true secret to successful microfarming is sustainability...both for the land, and for the microfarmer.

managers fixed the tomato prices for all the vendors, doing an enormous disservice to the public. To me, this meant two things. First, I was not going to be selling my tomatoes at that market for $4.00 each, regardless of size, and second, I was going to turn my tomatoes into value-added products and forget about peddling produce.

As my publisher, Mark Bailey, wrote in an email to me about the biodiversity of business, "One of the things I like most about environmentalism, in parallel with my business background, is the importance of diversity. It is as necessary in economics as it is in ecology." And

by steering away from monoculture crops and by using organic and near-organic farming practices, we can benefit the environment and have a sustainable microfarm.

If ever there was a buzzword with a dubious definition, it's "sustainability." Even Wikipedia notes, "A universally accepted definition of sustainability remains elusive." For a microfarm, sustainability essentially means growing crops in such a way that you don't exhaust the capacity of your land, or poison it. This is all well and good, and it's up to each farmer to decide how to do this and whether or not such organic no-nos as artificial fertilizers are evil for crops grown in containers. But I think the word has a deeper meaning, one that's partly about money and mostly about happiness.

The sustainability I'm writing about is your own, and that of your family, and whether or not all the work you are putting into your microfarm is rewarding you both financially and personally. For me, it's a no brainer because I've been growing plants since I was eight years old. It makes me happy to do this every year, regardless of the money. I'm turning seeds into food, and whether I sell the food or consume it, gardening or microfarming is a satisfying part of my life and always will be.

But for potential microfarmers who have no previous gardening or farming experience, having a microfarm may be boring, or worse yet, a big pain in the ass. And since my definition of sustainability includes happiness, you may have to just give it a try and see if you like it. I'm a firm believer in the bang-your-head-against-the-wall philosophy, which means if something bothers you or hurts you mentally or physically, it feels so good when you stop. If you give microfarming a try and you don't like doing it, or you find something better, then just stop it or go back to basic gardening.

But if you like what you're doing, and it's rewarding you both financially and mentally— *sustaining* you—go ahead and brainstorm that expansion plan.

RESOURCES

Suggested Reading

Taste, Memory: Forgotten Foods, Lost Flavors, and Why They Matter, by David Buchanan. Chelsea Green Publishing, 2012. This book is entirely about David Buchanan's search for the right microfarm, the right crops, and the right value-added products.

American Terroir: Savoring the Flavors of Our Woods, Waters, and Fields, by Rowan Jacobsen. Bloomsbury USA, 2010. An excellent book for understanding how the concept of *terroir*—the taste of place—can be incorporated into farms of any size.

Backyard Market Gardening: The Entrepreneurs Guide to Selling What You Grow, by Andy Lee and Patricia Foreman. Good Earth Publications, 2007. This book is precisely what the title says it is, and it provides good information from the basics to sustainable food systems. The only information lacking here is anything about value-added products.

Mini Farming: Self-Sufficiency on 1/4 Acre, by Brett L. Markham. Skyhorse Publishing, 2010. A good guide to growing crops in small spaces, and its value-added products are made with traditional preservation techniques like pickling and canning.

Seed and Plant Sources

Cross Country Nurseries
Janie Lamson has the best selection of live chile pepper, tomatoes, and eggplants for your microfarms. Of course, the plants cost more than growing them from seed yourself, but if a sudden influx of grasshoppers or a virus decimates part of your farm, who you gonna email? ChilePlants.com

Park Seed
Yes, they are a large seed supplier, but they are reasonably priced, have a good selection, and are prompt with delivery. ParkSeed.com

Seed Savers Exchange
These fine folks preserve heirloom seeds, grow them out, and save the seeds, just like their name suggests. I've always had great luck with their seeds. SeedSavers.org

Native Seeds/SEARCH
I like these folks in Tucson so much I've supported some of their specialty crops (like chile varieties) with donations. NativeSeeds.org

Tools That Dave Likes

Ames 16-Tine Double Play Bow Rake
I like this rake because one side of it loosens soil and the other side smooths it.
Excellent for working with gravel, too. Ames.com

Neuton Battery Mowers
I like my Neuton lawnmower because there's no gasoline or power cords, just
a very strong battery. And it's very quiet. NeutonPower.com

Weston Food Dehydrator
My ten-tray unit works very well, and is gentle on herbs. WestonSupply.com

Worx Aerocart
A combination garden cart/wheelbarrow with two wheels, dolly, and fulcrum,
this is a great combo unit for any microfarm. Worx.com

About Dave DeWitt

Declared the "pope of peppers" by *The New York Times*, Dave DeWitt is one of the foremost authorities in the world on chile peppers and spicy foods. After working his way through undergraduate and graduate school as a radio announcer, including a stint at top-rated WRVA radio in Richmond, Virginia, Dave owned audio/video production companies in both Richmond and Albuquerque, New Mexico. However, Dave's interest in chile peppers led to his writing numerous articles on the subject, and in 1984, St. Martin's Press published his book, *The Fiery Cuisines*, co-authored with Nancy Gerlach. In 1988, Dave and Nancy launched *Chile Pepper* magazine, which led to book projects including *The Whole Chile Pepper Book* (Little, Brown, 1990). Other best-selling books include *The Pepper Garden*, *The Hot Sauce Bible*, *The Chile Pepper Encyclopedia*, *The Spicy Food Lover's Bible*, and *The Complete Chile Pepper Book*. Dave and his wife, Mary Jane Wilan, are the founders of the National Fiery Foods and Barbecue Show, now in its 27th year. They live in the South Valley of Albuquerque with a Doberman, two Cornish Rex cats, and their microfarm.

Index

About Torrey House Press

The economy is a wholly owned subsidiary of the environment, not the other way around.
    —Senator Gaylord Nelson, founder of Earth Day

Love of the land inspires Torrey House Press and the books we publish. From literature and the environment and Western Lit to topical nonfiction about land related issues and ideas, we strive to increase appreciation for the importance of natural landscape through the power of pen and story. Through our 2% to the West program, Torrey House Press donates two percent of sales to not-for-profit environmental organizations and funds a scholarship for up-and-coming writers at colleges throughout the West.

Torrey House Press
Visit www.torreyhouse.com for reading group discussion guides, author interviews, and more.